SHANE

David Taylor

SHANE by David Taylor

Published by Glasshouse Publications Ltd

2201805001

This book is based on the life, experiences and recollections of Shane Almond
(aka Shane Taylor), Maz Taylor, Rob Foley, Andy Smith, Dean English, Paul Venis
and others. In some cases names of people, places, dates, sequences or the detail of
events have been changed to protect the privacy of others. Those interviewed have
stated to the publishers that their stories are truthful accounts.

SHANE: A FULL FEATURE DOCUMENTARY FILM WILL BE RELEASED THIS YEAR

For details see
www.glasshousemedia.co.uk
info@glasshousemedia.co.uk

First published in Great Britain in 2019 by Glasshouse Publications Ltd.
Waterside, 30 Town Wall, The Headland, Hartlepool, TS24 0JQ
www.glasshousepublications.com

Book ISBN: 978-1-9160907-0-5

A CIP record of this book is available from the British Library

Typeset in Palatino Linotype by Emma Taylor-Anderson

Cover by Tony Anderson

Cover photograph by Ian McCann 2018

Printed and bound in Great Britain by Print to Demand,
1 Newlands Road, Westoning, Bedfordshire, MK45 5LD

SHANE

as told to

David Taylor

Acknowledgements

The author and publishers would like to thank the following:

The Governor and HMP Holme House for their kindness
in letting us interview prison officers and allowing
us to film in the prison.

Police officers, magistrates and social workers
who contributed to the book.

The extensive numbers of prisoners and ex-cons who were
happy to share their memories on camera. For Shane's family
and friends who spent long hours giving interviews and
collaborating their accounts of his darkest days.
The large number of people from The Royal Arms estate
in Peterlee who welcomed us into their homes and shared their
memories of the events in this book.

To those who did not want their names mentioned but were
happy to check the book for any inaccuracies.

To Nicky Gumbel and Mark Elsdon-Dew and all at HTB
for their kindness and support.

Amanda Elsdon-Dew for editing the book and getting to grips
with the North-East dialect, accent, and slang.

For Sam and Ethena

In memory of Eddie Baker

1946 - 2019

FOREWORD

The Home Office keeps a list of the most dangerous prisoners in England's jails. In 2002, Shane Taylor was in the top six and he was still only 21 years old.

If Shane moved into your prison, as governor you had to ensure everyone was completely briefed on the danger he posed and implement your highest security protocols. Unlike some others, the danger wasn't that he would escape; it was that he was going to try to kill your prison officers. Because of what happened in his first prison, maximum safeguards had to be employed, with absolutely no physical contact allowed with guards, staff or inmates. Food had to be placed in a hatch that could only be opened if the outer door was locked. The minimal furniture in his cell was made of cardboard and he was locked up for 23 hours a day in solitary confinement. Legally, under human rights legislation, he was entitled to one hour a day exercise. However it often didn't happen because the prison couldn't provide the necessary manpower. For Shane to be moved required seven prison officers to be fitted up with riot gear, face masks, shields, helmets and armour to escort him from his cell inside the specialist unit to his exercise cage, a tiny, heavily protected space for one.

Yet even under such control measures Shane Taylor still managed to fight back and came close to killing an officer despite blows being rained down on him from the truncheons and shields of the other guards. Any mistake a guard made would be ruthlessly exploited. He was a man that seemed destined to kill and remain in prison for all of his natural life, until one day something happened that changed everything.

Shane's life prompts obvious questions that should impact on our society as a whole. How does a man become a monster? What can change a person? And if change is really possible, what should we do to offer help to those caught up in crime, drugs and violence?

Obviously in writing Shane's story some small liberties have been taken. No one can accurately remember actual conversations from years ago, so these parts of the narrative are reconstructed from the events and interviews with those who were there. Out of respect to people who were subjected to extreme violence, names have been changed in order to minimise the stress they may experience when reading this book. Equally some characters are composite figures made from combinations of real people where we need to hide their identities.

However, it is important to understand that all these events really happened and are transcribed from interviews with all the leading characters. Since the book is aimed at a wide audience, we have taken a view that the language will adhere roughly to the standards of international PG films but we must point out that this is a true story and recounts some extremely violent incidents. They are not invented or exaggerated but written down from the accounts of those who were there.

David Taylor

ONE

MAY 1980

MAZ

Maz picks herself up from the floor, her head is bleeding down the side of her face, her sides hurt when she tries to gulp in air, and her shoulder burns fiercely with pain. She grabs the side of the sofa for support and then hears the front door slam shut. She presumes he has gone back to the pub. Her glass coffee table top has shattered into small, sharp, gleaming squares and is all over the carpet, the cheap chrome frame is lying upside down, feet in the air.

She hauls herself into the chair next to her. Slowly her crying reduces to racking sobs. Her hands go protectively to her belly, although it is too soon for her to show, never mind for her to feel anything moving inside. The downstairs rooms of the house have been knocked into one via an archway through the brick wall. The kitchen stands at one end, the living area at the other. It seemed like a good idea at the time, but the demolition was carried out with far greater enthusiasm than the subsequent building work.

Maz lifts up her top and looks down at her ribs; they are incredibly sore and the bruises are starting to rise up. She takes a deep breath and the sharp stabbing pain doubles her up. A wave of nausea sweeps over her and she looks down at the car battery lying on its side next to her. The acrid smell reaches her as it leaks out on to the threadbare carpet. He threw it at her, picking it up at random from the pile of dismantled car parts piled up on the kitchen worktop.

She sits back in a daze and her mind floats free as if she is a viewer watching it all happen on the telly to someone else. She is only 19; her husband Stephen Almond is ten years older. They live in Middlesbrough in an old terraced house. She's here all the time; Stephen is only here when he's not in jail. She looks into the kitchen as if seeing it for the first time.

The worktop stretches from the tall fridge, past the window to the sink, and then on to the doorway. It is filled with things that Stephen is working on. The newspapers under the oily spare parts do little to stop the grime and oil from spreading. The lino on the floor is filthy and torn in places. Stephen's footprints have trodden the muck into the living room, his large shoes leaving clear outlines on the carpet. He is an immense man, thickset and strong.

He had never beaten her before, that is until she told him she was pregnant. She stupidly expected him to be pleased, but he reacted with fury, now the beatings are frequent, but never before like this, never has he lost it so completely. Maz knows he could do anything, she sees it in his eyes, his face, his utter lack of control. A wave of fear grabs her and pulls her attention back.

She pants, hard, short, small breaths trying to get air in her lungs without breathing in too deeply. Her ribs must be cracked or fractured. Another wave of dizziness sweeps over her and she starts exploring the damage to the side of her head. Her hand comes away with dark, sticky blood from her hairline, the flow still coming strong from the wound, and her top is now covered in blood. She starts cursing him with every breath, a constant stream of names, but even that becomes too much effort. She moans again, then tries to stand so she can get to the mirror and check how bad it is. It is easier said than done, her legs give way and she drops back into the armchair. Suddenly the door slams open and he is there again, he hasn't left the house at all and he is still in a rage.

'You stupid cow.'

His fist strikes out, hitting her already damaged shoulder, Maz cries out in pain. His face is livid, his dark matted hair soaked in sweat.

'Is it mine?'

His face is now pushed into hers, his spittle flecks on her brow. Her hands come up automatically to protect her eyes but he bats them away.

'Is it mine?' he screams again and then his fist swings wide and round into her, smashing straight into the top of her cheek, which tears open as she hears and feels the crack to her bone, like a spike biting deep inside. Maz feels like a rag doll. Her left eye goes out of focus and she feels like she is going to be sick. He doesn't stop; she thought the rage had burnt itself out, that this was the tail end of the storm, but she was very wrong.

He grabs a handful of hair and pulls her down on

7

to the floor. He drops on top of her legs, and starts pummelling his fists into her stomach over and over.

She throws up, vomit like a fountain shoots up, splashing Stephen in the face and then falling back down on her. The smell is enough to peel wallpaper, a rancid mix of half digested food, booze, bile and fear. He growls in disgust at the liquid dripping from him. It seems to ramp up his anger yet again. There are no limits to it now, he is past all that; she understands just how little her life might be worth and that of the baby just starting to grow inside her. Maz fully believes that she is going to die.

She screams again but knowing it won't help. In the last weeks the neighbours have heard it all before. Things get thrown, things get broken, but then they make up. People who have tried to help sometimes only find themselves turned on by Maz as well as Stephen. The police know it's not worth getting involved; Maz never wants to press charges. If calls come in, 'trouble at the Almonds' house', it's logged as just a domestic. If there is someone in the area, they might check it out.

However, if the police have any intelligence reports at hand suggesting that there are stolen goods in the house, that's different, they turn up mob handed because once it is declared as a crime scene they can search the house without a warrant.

So Maz screams, she screams in fear, she screams in pain and she screams in desperation but she also screams because she knows that no one is coming to help. Stephen gets up and stands over her. Now he's kicking and stamping. Things feel loose inside her. He looks around and sees the chainlink dog leash on the worktop. He picks it up and turns it into a whip, thrashing down on her. The end of the lead cuts into her and she tries to crawl over the carpet towards the door. Her upper arms bear bright red weals that start bleeding; a flap of skin hangs loose.

'I asked you, is it bloody mine?'

She would have said yes if she could speak but she can't say anything now. Her screams have turned into a rasping noise, her left eye is swollen shut, her lips split and she runs her tongue over broken teeth as she tries to spit.

'You want to be out, you bitch?' He grabs her hair again and this time drags her into the hallway. He opens the cupboard under the stairs and bundles her in, lifting her feet in the air and rolling her backwards into a heap. She tries to get back out of the cupboard as best she can, scrambling half out of the door. His fist flies out again and she loses consciousness.

Something is happening, she is moved this way and that, something deep inside her screams, then she realises that it is actually her. Then blackness. Maz comes round to a terrible pain deep inside, she can feel her trousers are now around her ankles and her bare backside is splintered by the rough wooden floor of the cupboard. He stands in the doorway, face triumphant, sporting a huge leering smile. There is blood dripping from his hand. He too is panting for breath now, the madness might not have passed but it is no longer fury that drives him on: it is something that may be even worse. He has a determined look on his face now; he has a plan. She lies gasping for breath as he leaves. She cannot understand what has happened, what he has done to her, she cannot move, she only hopes that it is finally over, until she sees what he has in his hands. He is back from the kitchen with a hammer and nails.

'No! No!'

She tries to scream again, she knows that she's dead if he hits her with the hammer. It is huge with a wicked claw at one end. He swings it over her head and she waits for the final assault, for the blackness to take her again, but he isn't aiming at her. He is hammering away at a pipe on the wall. She is confused, a ball of pain, everything is in agony. The last hammer blow moves the pipe from the wall and she can hear a hissing noise. The door is slammed shut, pushing her further back under the bottom of the stair treads. Then the hammering starts again and a nail splinters through the wooden frame of the door. He's nailing her in; she is sealed in the cupboard and then, before she passes out, she realises that the broken pipe is the main gas feed for the house. She starts to gag at the smell filling the cupboard and then knows no more.

*

When Maz comes round she cannot move at all, the ceiling above isn't hers, she tries to move her head but she can't, it's secured in a brace. Pain is everywhere; burning, sharp pains that pierce her when she tries to move, insistent throbbing pains when she lies still. A nurse's face appears over her.

'Well, you've been in the wars, haven't you?'

She disappears.

Maz can't speak though she's desperate to try; she has only one question that she needs to ask, only one question that has any meaning.

'Is my baby still alive?'

TWO

JUNE 1980

PETERLEE

PC Renwick, a woman in plainclothes, is driving the car; Maz is in the passenger seat. She rests her head against the glass as she looks out. The cool but hard surface seems to give relief to the swelling on her temple but is uncomfortable at the same time. This town looks very different to her terraced house in the heart of Middlesbrough. There the old brick houses were laid out in terraces around where the factories once stood. Here the houses are laid out in the middle of green spaces, they have flat roofs and white wooden walls. They look like the very embodiment of modern living but, as Maz starts to look closer, she sees that the paint is peeling off the exterior cladding on many of the houses, laying bare the pale, distressed and rotten woodwork underneath. On some estates the gardens are overgrown, and many of the fences are half down. The newest estates seem the best but, there again, they would. They are doing the tour around the town. PC Renwick is determined to talk the place up.

'It's only a mile from the beach, do you like the seaside?'

'Do they have sand or is it all pebbles? '

Renwick falls quiet, not really wanting to get

drawn into how the coal slurry from the collieries is dumped over the cliffs, turning them into vast alien landscapes.

She goes on cheerfully, 'The town's named after a local miners' leader, from years ago, Peter Lee.' She pauses, then loses some of her grim determination to keep things positive, 'Coal's everything around here, it's even how they name new towns.'

She seems bitter. It is the first time she is giving anything away of her own opinions, rather than sounding like a temp guide working for the tourist board.

Maz picks up on it.

'You don't like the place yourself, do you?'

Renwick gives a ruthful smile.

'I'm a Murton girl.'

'Is that one of the villages round here?'

'Yeah. At least until my mam and dad broke up, then I had to move here as a kid.'

Maz pushes. 'Had to?'

Renwick is at a junction and peers right for any oncoming traffic.

'They stopped all the new builds in the colliery villages once Peterlee was started, slapped a D Notice on all of them. If anyone needed to move out of the house for any reason, then they had to come here. There was nowhere else.'

'What happens if a lass gets preggers? She can't stay where she's brought up?'

'No, anyone who needs a house has to move here.'

'So it's a dumping ground for people like me?'

Renwick manages to be conciliatory.

'No, that's not fair, it's just that they have room for people with problems.'

Maz tries to look nonchalant but fails.

'So…' She goes on slowly and cautiously, 'Once I'm on my feet do you think I could get a house for me and the bairn here?'

Renwick smiles.

'Do you know Maz, I think you just might.'

Maz looks like the cat that's got the cream. Renwick can't help herself and ploughs on, 'It was built on the green farmland that separated the black pit heaps of the collieries.'

'You like your politics, don't you?'

'Don't be silly. Police officers don't do politics, besides I'm a liberal.'

Maz doesn't really know what to make of that, if it was a joke it's failed. She falls silent watching out the window. She takes in the trees and the wooded denes that intersect with the town and wonders what it all looked like before the mines, before the new town.

They turn into another estate; each one, she has noticed, is dominated by a totally different design to the others.

Something catches Maz's eye as they drive past.

'Why have they done that?'

She points out a house in the street with a pointy roof while all the rest are flat. The house has new windows and front door too.

Renwick laughs.

'It's the first sign of Thatcher's new "right to buy": new doors, double-glazing and a pitched roof on the top. The bloke who originally designed the houses used to live in Malta. He liked all the white houses out there that had flat roofs and glittered in the sun.'

Maz erupts with laughter. 'Silly sod didn't realise that we get rain not sunshine?'

'No Maz, he didn't, you're smarter than him.'

They fall into a more comfortable silence.

PC Renwick turns the car into a street set back from the main road.

Eventually Maz can't stop herself from asking what has been bothering her all along their journey.

'How do I know he won't find me here?'

Even after three weeks, two of them in hospital, Maz still has black eyes, now turned into reds, yellows, and blues as they heal. She still has bandages and dressings on some of her injuries.

'No one knows but our domestic violence unit.'

'Yeah, well, no one apparently knows where the Middlesbrough refuge is either, but I saw him standing over the road, looking in.'

'I know Maz, we had it confirmed.'

The car pulls up in front of a house in the middle of

the row. The car is plain, it has no markings, it's about five years old, scuffed and as nondescript as it was possible to be, no one would look at it twice, just like the house before them, nothing out of the ordinary.

'Trust me, you're safe here.'

Renwick looks at Maz intently and grabs her hands.

'In Middlesbrough the refuge has been going a long time, people talk, even women who should know better, or sometimes they are seen in town and followed, but it's not like that here.'

Maz pulls away.

'So, is this it? '

Renwick smiles.

'Yeah, great isn't it.'

Maz doesn't reply but you can see she is pleased. There are houses on either side of the street but there are gardens and green spaces all around, including some trees that must have been there decades before the houses were built.

Renwick is pleased at Maz's reaction. 'It isn't the Ritz but it's good. Come on, let's go in.'

They are about to get out of the car when the policewoman's radio sparks to life from inside her jacket. She takes it out but shields it from view.

'Control to PC one five six two, call when free to talk, over.'

PC Renwick presses a button then pushes the phone back deep into her pocket.

'Come on, let's go in.'

Maz gets out the car; she only has a carrier bag with her.

They knock and wait, a curtain window twitches as someone looks out and then the door opens, they go inside.

Maz is met by a tough-looking woman with short spiky hair who takes in at a glance the nature of Maz's injuries.

'I'm Julie; they said you were coming, come on in and let me show you to your room.'

Maz is slightly hesitant.

'I don't have any clothes or things, I had to leave everything, I've got nothing for the bairn when it comes either.'

Maz looks uncomfortable.

Julie's tough face breaks into a smile and she throws her arms around Maz.

'Don't worry, pet, we'll sort you out.'

Julie moves up the hallway and Maz follows.

When they leave, PC Renwick lingers in the front room and calls in on her radio. The control desk asks her to wait while she is put through to the duty inspector.

'You're there safe and sound? '

'Yes, just got her booked in.'

'Good job, we've had a call out, someone has just been nicked breaking into the Middlesbrough refuge and smashing the place up.'

'Is it Stephen Almond?'

'I don't know yet, officers are attending now.'

'If it's him, throw away the key, will you?'

'I wish.'

*

The months go by. In early December, on a grey, cold and rainy day when the winter is just starting to bite, her husband catches up with her again back in Middlesbrough while she is staying with a friend for a few days. A next door neighbour hears the screams and summons up the courage to call the police. When they arrive they find Maz sprawled on the floor. Her injuries are horrific; the first policeman on the scene runs back out of the house and stands in the rain doubled up as he vomits on to the dead weeds in the garden. Maz is rushed off to the emergency department at the hospital. The police are stationed on guard at the entrance to the ward. They are waiting for news. If the baby is born dead, they have already cleared with the Crown Prosecution Service for her husband to be arrested on a charge of manslaughter although a strong case is also being made for it to be upgraded to murder because he had a clear intention to kill the baby. They wait through the night.

Early morning comes and as an officer thankfully takes a hot cup of coffee from a nurse as the shift changes, a scream can be heard from the next room.

Someone is dangling a healthy baby boy upside down, giving him an old fashioned welcome to this world by smacking his bum in order for him to take his first breath.

It is 12th December 1980. At ten past six in the morning, baby Shane is born, very much alive and kicking.

THE ROYAL ARMS

It is a year and a half later and Maz is a happy woman.

The Royal Arms estate is the oldest part of Peterlee; here the houses are conventionally built, brick, post-war constructions, the same as those found in council housing estates in hundreds of towns and villages across the country. The oldest houses in the town have become the harder to rent at least until people come to realise just how poor the new factory built system houses are. They are shipped in with concrete walls and flat roofs to be assembled on site like children's toys. However the concrete is substandard, the insulation proves to be non-existent and the reputation of the town continues to drop like a stone. Maz, however, is happy on The Royal Arms estate; the council rehoused her after a few months in the women's refuge, just after the birth of her little Shane in December 1980.

The people in the town name the estate after the iconic pub The Royal Arms that stands next to the local shops. The pub itself has something of a reputation. Even some of the locals use it warily; strangers do come in occasionally, usually accompanied by a regular. These newcomers often become involved, whether they like it or not, in a game of 'who do you think you are looking at' with the inevitable outbreak of trouble.

*

When Shane is one year old, the past eventually catches up with Maz yet again. Stephen Almond has found out where they are living and is coming towards the house.

Maz has always lived in fear that this day will come.

She sees him as he walks up the path. He is trying to look through the window but the light is reflecting on the glass and he can't see inside. Maz has already grabbed Shane and taken him upstairs before her husband can get to the front door. There is one other thing that she grabbed before she left the living room, the poker from the fireplace.

She thunders back down the stairs, iron poker still gripped hard in her hand. It is two foot long and half an inch thick. The handle sits in her hand as if it is a sword. Her husband's outline can be seen through the obscure glass as he hammers on the door. She is terrified, utterly terrified. The big bad wolf is outside and about to start trying to blow the house down.

'Open up Maz, it's me.'

His voice is slurred; he has been drinking.

His open hand rattles the glass panel in its frame as he strikes it again.

Maz sees that the chain isn't on and quickly tries

to fasten it. The heavy links drop into place the very moment that Stephen's shoulder hits the door and it bursts open, nearly knocking her over. She needn't have bothered with the chain, not only has the door lock broken, the chain has pulled out the screws on the door frame. He is in.

He swings his punch: straight out of the block with no preamble and no warning. Instinctively Maz swings the poker up towards his oncoming hand to protect herself. It catches him on his inner forearm behind the wrist, right on the bone and this time it is he who screams out in pain. She wildly swings the poker back and forth, forcing him back out of the door.

Standing on the landing at the top of the stairs little Shane silently grips the baby gate, his ginger hair pushing through the bars as he tries to see what is going on.

Outside Stephen is scrambling backwards as Maz holds the poker above her head.

Maz yells at him, 'Do you want some more of this?'

She might be sounding tough but she can hardly stop herself from running.

'When are you going to give it up? He is yours, you idiot… anyhow he was… but he's not now, he's just mine.'

He sounds surprised at her certainty.

'He is mine? Really?'

He pauses.

'…But he's ginger.'

She doesn't know if that is a joke; he can be like that at times, dry.

'There's ginger in my family.'

'I saw you and Stan in the pub laughing behind my back.'

'So bloody what, I like a laugh.'

'Aye, well I thought it was his, you know.'

'Well it wasn't, I wouldn't touch him with a barge pole.'

He half smiles at her.

'Yes you would.'

She doesn't smile back but gives a slight nod.

'Aye, well maybe I would, but I didn't.'

'I think you've broke my arm.'

'You broke my door.'

Maz is frozen in place, poker in hand, heart beating like a drum waiting for him to attack. It doesn't happen.

'I'll go then.'

She nods.

'Aye, and don't come back.'

'No, I won't,' he agrees, and slouches off down the street.

Surprisingly he keeps his word, and she doesn't see him again for decades.

GORDON

Maz and Gordon Taylor have been living together for the last two and a half years. He is the exact opposite of Stephen. He is calm and gentle, whereas Stephen Almond had been manic and violent. Maz's divorce has now come through and her old husband is in the past for good. However, when Maz and Gordon sit Shane in front of them and tell him they have decided to get married, it isn't for conventional reasons.

It starts with an envelope.

Here the story becomes murky, memories are vague, maybe somewhat conveniently.

What is for sure is that Maz had got hold of a letter that was not meant for her but for her neighbour. According to Maz it tumbled through her front door like manna from heaven, and she opened it without, she claimed, looking at the name on the front of the envelope. Maybe there was more to it, maybe it was taken from the neighbour's house just after the postman arrived, maybe it was sticking out of the letterbox just enough for it to be pulled back out. There again, maybe it was stolen from the post office and sold on the black market. It's hard to tell. Everyone is at it; everyone is either pinching things or buying dodgy items from a lad down the pub.

Whatever the real story, when Maz sees what's in the envelope she can't believe her luck.

She is skint again, out of fags and can't afford a decent night out in the pub, and here suddenly in her hand is a brand new credit card. The fact that the name on it isn't hers isn't a problem.

Well, it isn't going to hurt anyone, is it? Her neighbour will tell her bank she never received it and the credit card company will be the only one to lose out. They have enough money; they won't even miss it.

In those days you had to ring in to authenticate the card. How her neighbour's personal details were obtained by Maz to answer the necessary security questions is anyone's guess. Let's just draw a veil over that. However there are unwritten rules about these phone calls: you don't ring the credit card company to initiate them from your own phone, you use the public one in The Royal Arms.

There's a spring in her step as she figures out just what she wants to buy. You have to do things fast, it won't be long before they know it's stolen and put a block on it. A new leather jacket, a new video player; she gets the shopping list together in her head. 'A few treats, a few things to sell on for some cash. Of course you must be sensible, you can't get things that have to be delivered to the house like a washing machine because they can trace it back. No... best to go to the nearest big town like Sunderland, or Hartlepool, or maybe Middlesbrough...' Her interior dialogue with herself runs on. 'No,' she thinks, 'not the Boro, I'm known by too many people there. Sunderland it is then. Maybe I'll get a taxi back, the driver can help me with everything that I've bought.'

Maz shouldn't be skint; she's been on a good run lately. She's experimenting with her benefit giro checks. It's difficult but, if you are clever and extremely careful, you can change the amounts on them. You have to stay within the bounds of reason. You can't make them into mega thousands; that would never work. The woman in the post office never really looks, and if you aren't too greedy you can get away with an extra hundred or so every time. Happy days.

She kisses Gordon on the cheek and looks down at Shane.

'Do what Daddy Gordon says, you hear? And don't run away.'

She turns to Gordon.

'Keep your eyes peeled, you know what he's like.'

'I will.' He starts to cuddle little Shane into him on the sofa.

'Gerroff.' Shane breaks free.

Maz shakes her head and leaves them: what will be will be.

Gordon has a drink from his can of Special Brew and puts his feet up on the coffee table while he reads the sports section in the local paper. By the time Maz is at the front gate of the garden, Shane is over the fence at the back.

It's later on in the day; Maz is in The Royal Arms having a pint or two with her friend Shaz. Maz is wearing her new leather jacket with killer shoulder pads. It is black with a red collar and lining. She has a short black leather skirt to match and a black top, 'very sexy,' she thinks. Her permed hair is piled high and teased out into a halo. Maz figures she is a dead ringer for that woman off Dynasty on the telly. The young one that is, not the old slapper.

'Hey, Maz, that's a bonny jacket.'

Maz takes the compliment.

Another woman staggers towards her.

'Here, if you can afford that, you can afford to give me the money you owe me.'

'Sorry Pam, it was a prezzie from our Robert, wasn't it, Shaz, tell her.'

'Aye Pam, she's skint, it was from Robert; he called round this afternoon, I saw him.'

Pam knows when she's being lied to, she's thinking about making a fuss but Maz is staring her out. She takes a passing shot as she staggers away to her table at the other side of the pub.

'You're a ruddy liar you, you cow.'

Maz gives her the finger and turns back to Shaz, they giggle like kids. Shaz takes a large swig.

Maz looks out the window. 'I haven't a clue where Shane is.'

Shaz laughs and says, 'He'll turn up when he's good and ready.'

Shane has gone out on the go-cart that Gordon had built for him. In many ways he's a good man, he tries to be a dad for Shane. It's a shame that he doesn't really know what makes a good dad, and then Shane is difficult, a cute kid but wild. He has been out on his cart since Maz went out on her shopping spree.

Horden, a pit village, stands on top of the cliffs overlooking the cold North Sea. Above it is Peterlee, built on the top of the hill that rises up rapidly from the edge of the village below. Shane is sitting in his go-cart looking down the 200-foot incline to the houses in the distance.

He doesn't know it but the field he is in belongs to a different town and different people. Beneath the wheels of his cart lies the old medieval village of Yoden, destroyed by Vikings in 900 AD, long before the Norman Conquest. The bumps in the field probably indicate significant remains, no one has ever checked. However it's a great place to play.

Shane looks down the field to Horden far below. To Shane the 200-foot incline seems like an ideal spot to race down in a go-cart. There have been others who have done it; people have talked about those fearless or stupid enough to try.

Fortunately Shane is thrown out half way down and rolls to a halt, before the cart hits the fence at the bottom with a loud smack. He sits on the grass looking down at the wheel that has come adrift from the cart. It's bent at an angle, broken off when it hit the rock that made him go head over heels.

He rummages in his pocket and finds the packet of cigarettes and box of matches he stole earlier from his mam's bag.

Everyone seems to think smoking is a good idea. His mam opens her eyes in the morning and has a ciggie in her mouth before taking her second waking breath. Gordon has one in his mouth all the time – often unlit, waiting, because he is pacing himself. It sticks there as if glued to his bottom lip. Shane loves watching him talk, the cigarette bobs up and down as he speaks, held in place by some strange power born of spit and balance.

He sticks a cigarette in his own mouth and tastes the tobacco. Maz doesn't often use filters; well, it depends on whom she's cadged a packet from really. It is a bitter taste and the texture of the dried leaf is strange on his tongue. It tingles a bit and is exciting. Even to a four year old, he knows that this is a marker of something, a rite of passage that moves him inches from his world and into theirs.

He has never struck a match before but he has watched carefully when others have done it. It is a still day, there is no wind, when he strikes, and it flares straight into life.

He holds the match and stares at the flame. He can feel the heat as he brings it near his face, but he still doesn't try to light the cigarette. Had he seen himself at that point, he would have seen something of Gordon, the unlit fag in his mouth held in place by the spit to his dry lip. The flame burns down near his fingers and he throws it down on the ground. The field is dry and some of the grass slowly catches fire. He stamps it out and takes out another match.

The sun is setting behind him further up the hill and the light dims. This time, although fascinated by the flame, he lights the cigarette and takes a deep breath. Three things then happen at roughly the same time. First the flame on the match burns down towards his fingers, he coughs explosively, and then he drops the cigarette on his leg.

Pain strikes him, as his head seems to explode.

He then starts to feel sick and throws up.

The grass is smouldering at his feet but dies out by itself. His leg now has a burn on it just below his knee, it is a sharp pain and throbs like the beat of a drum. Given that no one is watching he starts to sob, just a little.

He knows that when his mam sees the burn she will know he has been smoking and pinched her tabs. He's going to get smacked, and hard. He sits there, totally miserable. He looks at the cart and knows he'll never be able to drag that back up the hill. Four years old, hurt, half lost and scared, but he stops crying.

In the pub Maz is having a grand time, Shaz is great company and, with some cash to splash, they are holding court with their friends. Just then Gordon sticks his head around the door.

'Maz, I've just seen a police car on Crawford Avenue, our Shane was in the back.'

Maz and Shaz scramble immediately.

Maz runs up the street, a police car is parked outside their house with one policeman in the driver's seat using his radio; the other is knocking on their door with Shane standing next to him. Maz runs up, barges past the policeman and grabs Shane.

'Where've you been, pet? We've been looking all over for you, haven't we, Gordon.'

Gordon doesn't run as fast as Maz and is older than her by about 12 years, in his mid -30s. He wheezes when he runs.

He manages to squeeze out a reply.

'Aye, we've been looking everywhere.'

Maz glares at the policeman.

'He hasn't done anything, what are you here for?'

The policeman takes in her 'going out for the night' clothes but holds back from commenting.

'Can we go inside please? We have to talk.'

His colleague has finished on the radio, presumably updating the control room on the arrival of Shane's parents, and comes up to the house as well.

'What's all this about?' Maz asks.

'Can we just go in, please?'

Maz pauses. 'Okay, but you're not going to use our loo, you lot use that as an excuse to have a nose about… or so I've heard anyway. Not that we've got anything to hide, mind you, it's just the principle of the thing, isn't it.'

The policeman smiles. 'Okay, I promise not to go to your loo, now can we come in, this is important.'

Reluctantly Maz agrees. She unlocks the door and goes straight into the living room, scooping up her special inks and pens and putting them in the sideboard.

'Ee, this place is a mess, I hope you don't mind.'

The policeman doesn't seem to see anything suspicious. Gordon comes in carrying Shane who looks terrified and defiant at the same time.

Maz turns and takes him out of Gordon's hands. She sees the large plaster on his leg.

'What have you done to him?' she shrieks.

Slowly the story comes out and is pieced together. Shane was found wandering the streets in Horden – a four year old, all alone, and in distress.

When an old man had asked him what was the matter, Shane said a bad man in a black car had taken him and burned him with cigarettes.

The policeman is caring and deeply concerned.

'We have all our cars out looking for this man. Every black car is being stopped on the coast road and through to Peterlee, but we worry that he has long gone. The police doctor has seen Shane and we think there is only one burn mark.'

He pauses, more deep concern on his face.

'We are going to take him to hospital but he was crying for you, so we called here first to take you with us.'

Maz cuddles Shane in tight

'Wasn't crying, mam, I wasn't,' he says.

The visit to the hospital passes without incident and eventually they are back in the house.

Maz takes Shane to bed and as she tucks him in says, 'Tell me the truth, Shane, you won't get wrong, I won't smack you, did a man really take you and burn you?'

'Yes, mam, I promise.'

It's the next night. After repeated attempts to establish the truth, Shane cracks and tells his mam what happened. She doesn't say anything and puts him to bed.

He can just about hear them downstairs as he lies in the dark.

There is laughter.

'The little cheeky sod.'

'I wonder how many people in black cars they have stopped?'

There are howls of laughter.

Shane lies in the dark and smiles.

*

A few weeks go by and then the same caring policeman is back at the door with another officer.

Maz stands there, Shane behind her. She doesn't invite them in.

Maz takes a deep breath from her cigarette and blows the smoke towards them.

'Have you caught the man who did it yet?'

The policeman isn't smiling; neither is the other officer standing next to him.

'Marion Almond, I'm arresting you for fraud...'

The rest of the 'reading of her rights' goes by in a daze until the punchline:

'...And we have a warrant to search these premises.'

They push past her and Shane and go inside, where they makes a beeline to the sideboard where she keeps her special giro-altering kit.

*

Which brings us back to the moment when Maz explains to a young Shane that she is going to have to go away for a few months.

'But first,' she says, 'Gordon and I are going to be married and he is going to become your proper daddy. You are going to get his name now. Your name is going to be Shane Taylor.'

She wraps her arms around him and cuddles him in.

'If we don't get married, pet, they'll take you into care, and we don't want that, do we? Gordon will look after you and you'll be here when I get back.'

She cuddles Shane again. He gets the concept of

the name change. Shane Taylor: he likes the idea of that a lot, sounds better than Almond, that's just an invitation to be labelled as a ginger nut.

FIVE

1987

LEISURE PURSUITS

The leisure centre stands a short distance away from the shops. Squat and rectangular, it sits at the top of a green hill rising up from the road that loops around the centre of the town. It has a concrete panelled base, and then a sun-faded, red turned pink, corrugated plastic roof perched on the top. It resembles a giant shoebox, with two long towering stainless steel chimneys rising up the side of the building outside the swimming pool. A second, taller shoebox structure behind it houses the squash courts, gymnasium, and five-a-side indoor pitches. Outside to the right the ground dips away into the car park then, beyond it, drops even further down into another tributary of the dene. A group of kids approach the entrance but only Shane goes through the doors. The others walk past the front of the building.

Shane is carrying a towel wrapped around his swimming trunks in a bundle under his arm; he pays and passes through a turnstile system.

He quickly makes his way to the far end of the centre where there is a fire door. He opens it fast and Dean and his other friends swarm in free of charge.

Their plan is to go swimming but Dean spots something on the way to the changing rooms. Dean is Shane's best pal. They started school together on the first day of term and hit it off straight away. They regard school as an optional extra at best, and usually ignore it altogether. They usually pretend to go to school before running away for the day.

Maz used to answer the complaints on the phone from the school with a simple question.

'What can you do? I brought him in, it's your job to hold on to him.'

Dean is as bad as Shane. The two six year olds are game for just about anything.

Dean is passing the telephone booth by the changing rooms when it catches his eye.

'Hey, Shane look at this.'

Shane comes over nonchalantly, careful not to be obvious. The booth has a canopy over the pay phone to give some small measure of privacy but the small boys are standing below that, level with the body of the phone mechanism and the box under it where the money is kept. They can see through a crack in the top of the box that it is full to the brim with coins. Dean runs his fingers around the top of the box; it's loose but still attached.

'If we had something to put in like a lever we could open this,' he says as he looks at Shane, 'we could! I've seen our Frankie do it before.'

Shane is impressed at Dean's wisdom on these matters.

'What's a lever?'

'Something like a screwdriver or that thing you use on bikes.'

Shane's face lights up as he remembers something. He dashes off, leaving Dean to guard their treasure and returns a few minutes later.

'So will this do then?' He pulls out a flat-bladed screwdriver from his pocket. 'It was in the bar next to the window, it's been there for ages.'

Dean grins.

'How did you know that?'

'Daddy Gordon sometimes drinks in the bar in here and brings me in with him, I've played with it before.'

Shane is as proud as punch at his memory and initiative.

For Dean it is as if he has pulled off a magic act second to none, and he recognises it's now his turn to act. The flat blade goes under the cover but he lacks the strength to lever it up.

'What are you doing?'

'I'm trying to break it open.'

'Don't you just take out the screws?'

A short while later with a valuable life lesson learned the top is off.

Now Dean and Shane are wandering around the centre with their pockets stuffed with coins. The bulges in their trouser pockets are so large and heavy they have to hold up their waistbands with one hand to stop them falling down, their jackets are distended and their side pockets hang down under the weight.

'It's no good, they'll see us if we go out like this.'

'We could use the drinks machine.'

'Brilliant!'

They attack all the vending machines with their bulging pockets; some of their proceeds are turned into food, drink and packets of cigarettes, which are packed away into whatever space they can find in their already full pockets. They carefully make their way with their misshapen shell suits to the fire escape door they used earlier. Coins leak behind them like a trail being left behind to mark their progress.

Just as they get there, a man blocks their way.

It is Mitch Williams, the assistant manager; he looms way above the kids.

'Gotcha.' He grabs Dean and Shane. 'Give me the money now.'

He is six foot two tall, with hair down to a buzz cut. He's a nice bloke, but terrifying to the kids.

Pockets are tipped out, and the cash and contraband is piled up on the floor. Mitch is astonished at how much there is, and then is suddenly faced with uncertainty about what to do with two crying six year olds.

Several people come out of the changing rooms and see him holding on to the young children. Mitch tries to explain.

'They've pinched money out of the phone booth.'

A granny looks over her glasses at him and glares.

'Hey, they're only bairns, man, look at them, you should be ashamed of yersel.'

Dean and Shane are small for their age and Mitch towers above them.

Another woman looks at him and tuts, but he is resolute. Tuts won't sway him from his duty.

'I'll have to get the police in.'

At that the two small boys howl and cry. They squirm in his grasp and he has to redouble his grip to hold on to them.

Tuts aside, it is now dawning on Mitch just how much trouble it is going to be to sort this out. Detaining crying children while he waits for the police to eventually leave their bacon sandwiches in the canteen, and then saunter across town to attend the scene of the crime, is all going to take time. The taking of witness statements from staff and customers, the management report he will have to make will be a nightmare, and then there is the ever-lurking fear that, somewhere down the road, a reporter is going ask him what he thought he was doing in depriving little children of their liberty.

Pragmatism rules the day. Mitch backs his bum into the handle of the fire doors and they spring open.

'Get out, you're banned, don't come back.'

Shane and Dean spring out into the car park.

They stand jumping up and down calling him names.

'Yeah, you tosser.' More abuse follows.

They make V signs, and then Dean drops his trousers down and bares his bum.

'Tosser.'

Mitch goes to run after them, they squeal and run off like the wind down past the car park and into the tree line where they disappear.

Inside the woods they stop in one of the makeshift camps where their schooldays are often spent.

For Shane, his eyes are alive to new possibilities; it's not just the money they nearly got away with, it's the buzz. The excitement tears at him and fills him, he is juiced up and he wants to feel like this again and again. The moment he was grabbed, the moment he got away, he was buzzing, ...BUZZING. He is jumping up and down, arms up, head back looking at the sky.

He looks at Dean. He gets it, he feels the same.

It is their first ever crime. It's not their last.

Even at six they are lateral thinkers: not everywhere will have a phone box, but...They pass the Methodist church which stands at the far end of the leisure centre car park, and go inside. The church is open and the minister inside is looking out of the window; he doesn't see the kids creeping in and making off with the collection box. Though it didn't have as much money as the leisure centre phone box it still gave the buzz. Had they known it, since it was a rather well made arts and crafts box carved out of satin wood, it would have fetched a tidy sum on the antique black market. If you are interested in it, it is probably still where they dumped it in the trees at the back of the church.

SIX

1987

SHOPS

It's as if a switch has been hit. A world of new possibilities is suddenly before them. Now Shane sees everything differently.

The very same week as the leisure centre, things roll into motion. How do kids instinctively know the things they know? Six and seven year olds are supposed to play with toys, have early bed-times; not self-organise into mini Bonnie and Clyde-style gangs. Maybe self-organise is a poor term. Shane would deny that anything was organised at all. He looks back and says it was just a bunch of friends firing each other up into acts of bravado. Now it is hard to imagine but as a child Shane was bullied and picked on until he reached about 15 or 16 years old. Even so he was one of those people that act as a catalyst on others. If someone had a daft idea, then Shane was up for it. He would run away from home for days on end and get away with it. While the same was true for other children on the estate, Shane was just so up for doing anything that others found themselves doing things that they wouldn't have done if they were by themselves. He was buzzed by the excitement, he was up for mischief and others hung around and joined in.

So…

A gang of young kids walk into Asda the biggest supermarket in town. At the side of the store there is a fire door. Two children wait outside it with empty supermarket trolleys, nervously kicking around a half brick in what looks like a makeshift game of football. They look like they are waiting for their mum.

The first kids into the supermarket go straight towards the fire door inside and wait. They look bored, just as young children should in supermarkets. Customers imagine their parents are in the next aisle.

The remaining kids split into two. A security guard shifts uneasily at sight of the kids; he suspects the little beggars are up to no good. One group lingers near the sweets. He knows they are going to try to pinch something, and starts towards them.

As he gets close he re-evaluates their ages.

'Strewth, they're young,' he thinks.

One of them sees him and gives a half smile. They all then turn and look at him. He thinks he hears a whistle, sounding like a referee signalling a kick off at a match. The kids in front of him grab the sweets and throw them at him and other customers. There is mayhem. He chases the little monsters but they all split up, an alarm sounds and he stops the chase in his tracks as he turns to the front doors of the store. He can't see anything happening there.

A plainclothes store detective runs past him to the rear of the store. Customers stand open mouthed. The fire doors are open; kids are piling videos and hi-fi units in the waiting trolleys outside.

Some slightly older boys are carrying the heavier audio equipment. Another empty trolley is rolled forward for them to use. Then the doors slam shut and they are off. Six trolleys are being pushed out of the town centre and on to the housing estate at speed by a host of six and seven year olds. By the time the security staff at the shop realise what happened they are all long gone. Shoplifting has now become a new art form, a hit and run attack, a minor league blitzkrieg.

Within weeks Maz is overwhelmed by her son's new crime lifestyle .

She even phones the police herself to report him once when he burgles his school and nicks some bikes. Shane had taken them to Maz's sister who sold them on for five pounds each. When they both later confess to Maz what has happened, she realises just how bad it could look. After all, with her record it could look as if she had organised things as a 'Fagin' type of operation. So she gets the bikes back and calls the police in. She thinks that it will teach Shane a lesson, and it did, but not the one she expected.

The policeman sits on her sofa drinking a cup of tea. Maz is so worried she even lets the other policeman go and use the loo, forgetting that was an open invitation for him to secretly search the house. The policeman with the apparently dodgy bladder comes back into the room and gives a slight shake of the head to the other officer; nothing to be seen.

Maz picks it up.

'Oh, that's great, I invite you here because something has to be done about Shane and here you are riffling through my drawers.'

Officer Weak Bladder protests.

'I've done no such thing. We don't do that.'

Maz scowls.

'So what are we going to do about him then?'

Shane sits nervously fidgeting on the other sofa.

The policeman says, 'We can't do nowt about it. He's too young.'

Maz fumes:

'Too young!'

Shane's face lights up, too young?

The police leave with the bikes.

Shane is dancing around the house,

'The police can't do nowt. I'm not old enough.'

Maz groans.

*

A bolt has now been fitted to the outside of the bedroom door and Shane is inside, and he is hammering on it.

'Lemme out.'

'No, You're grounded.'

The noise goes on for about an hour and Maz is on the verge of giving in, when suddenly it goes quiet. There is blissful silence. Maz's eyes are drawn to the clock; the second hand sweeps by. She wants to bask in the peace but knows there is a catch and can't quite relax. She pops a can open and switches on the telly to watch Steve Davis on the snooker, but keeps it on mute so she can hear what the little monster will do next. Something drops past her window with a loud thump.

'What the...?'

She gets up slowly to go to the window. Gordon is leaning forward with a puzzled expression, and then suddenly Shane drops past the window, then bounces up on his feet.

Maz gets there to see the mattress from his bed lying on the garden under his window, Shane is flashing V signs at her and runs away down the street.

He doesn't come back for four days. Everyone had been out looking for him. When he does return it is in the back of a police car; he was found ten miles away, stealing from someone's house. He has a broad smile on his face.

'The police can't do nowt. I'm not old enough.'

She bundles him up in her arms and takes him upstairs for a bath. She cannot bring herself to tell him off, or ask questions, she is so relieved he is safe. He has been away for four days... four days, for goodness sake. She holds him tight. The next day he runs away again. When he eventually comes back he finds they have now fixed the bedroom and tried to make it escape proof. The bolt is on the door, and now the window is nailed shut so he can't jump out.

Shane alternates between wrecking everything in the room and promising to be good. He wears them down when he makes more noise than they can bear and then promises to be good. He is first allowed downstairs and then, after a while, when he makes too much noise for them to take, given permission to go out to play. But play for Shane is not the same as it is for the other boys.

*

Years later Maz thinks back to those days, she says:

'I used to try and ground him. And the more I tried to ground him, the worse he got. He used to disappear all the time for days and days. I used to be at my wits' end, me. I used to be all over, looking the streets and hunting him down and everything. And when they brought him home, I couldn't punish him 'cos I was more relieved to see he was okay. Do you know what I mean? He was safe and sound, and I used to put him in the bath and then make him a hot meal, give him something to eat, and spoil him.'

SEVEN

RATS

For Shane and his friends at the tender age of nine, there is a cultural or social phenomenon happening around them. Call it what you will, it shapes the minds of his group of friends, and elevates some of the older lads to cult status. It creates and moulds his aspirations, setting in his mind how he can move from being the little lad, picked on and exploited by the older boys, to become someone with respect.

The helicopter overhead is the first sign of a chase. People stop what they are doing and flock outside, the local version of formula one is about to begin: the RATS are at it.

RATS stands for the 'Royal Arms Twoc Squad'. Everyone around Peterlee knows what a TWOCKER is. It's an acronym that comes from the legal definition of stealing a car: 'Taking Without the Owner's Consent'. Twocking is a thrill-seeking crime suddenly elevated to a spectator sport.

*

You are in the street and then you hear the beating of the blades getting closer. Helicopters are in the air, everyone goes quiet waiting for the next sound, that of an approaching over-revved car. It suddenly appears with kids hanging out of the windows, pumping their fists and rousing the crowds. Everyone cheers, they shout, they clap, as if at a concert. The car does handbrake turns, leaving skid marks on the Tarmac, soon the blues and twos are to be heard and the police patrols, aka 'bobby cars', or 'jam sandwiches' – the police cars with orange and yellow stripes on their sides – bring up the rear. First, maybe a single bobby car, then more and more join the affray. Sometimes there are up to 20 on a chase, with the chopper overhead, waiting for the moment the twockers dump the car. The local shops are raised up on a short parade above the main road. They are accessed either up a ramp or by short flight of steps. It is a perfect viewing platform and placed at a T-junction. The crowds come from the shops and fill the parade, everyone loves it.

The people on the estate don't exactly hold up scorecards but it isn't that far away from the truth. It sums up the attitude of the majority of people on the estate. Today many of those who were kids back then maintain that they had no awareness of it being wrong, it was just what people did.

*

One of the standard escape strategies of the TWOC squad is to try to drive up narrow pedestrian cuts between the houses; the police cars sometimes get stuck, and this, of course, is classed as a great result. Other times, they deliberately hit kerbs at high speed to try to tear off the under-chassis of the stolen car, and hope the police cars do the same. Often they try to drive down the stairs into pedestrian underpasses. Usually they try to get into the tree lines at the edges of the wooded valleys, or denes, that run up from the coast, and then spread out like the fingers of a hand into the centre of the town.

One lad is at the heart of the RATS and he decides to take things further.

He starts a chase somewhere on the main road, the A19, which runs past Peterlee. He is in a stolen car travelling at 90mph or faster, trying to get noticed. He goes backwards and forwards, turning at the slip-road junctions, and coming back down the other side of the road. He might have to wait a while before he passes someone on duty. This time it takes him an hour or so, screeching back and forth down the A19 a few miles either side of the town until at last a police car spots him.

He can imagine the conversation in the jam sandwich. First, they will be calling him every name under the sun, while they are checking with their control by radio who the car belongs too. As soon as it comes up notified as being stolen, their blue lights come on, and their sirens sound out their two-tone howl. Once they give chase he comes off the main road and spins down the side roads around the town. He is not ready yet; he is waiting for the sound of more sirens.

When he hears more cars joining the chase he dodges around and suddenly shoots off back to The Royal Arms estate. If he can do it fast enough, through enough twists and turns, he can get far enough ahead of the chasing car to do what he wants. He gets to a crossroad and does a skidding handbrake turn so he is now facing the oncoming police car. He holds the centre of the road; one foot stomped down on the accelerator, the other keeping the clutch down. It is held on the handbrake while the car screams in protest. He starts to dip the clutch and the back wheels spin and burn smoke. The police car driver seems in a quandary; if the joyrider wants to shoot past him, he will need to go over the grass verges, but there are people and loads of children flocking towards the cars. The police car brakes and swings sideways across the road to block his path.

The boy driving the stolen car has engineered it into this position. His favourite film, The *Blues Brothers*, is now ten years old, but he loves watching the video over and over again. It has stunning scenes of car crash carnage. In his mind's eye he might as well be in Chicago. He floors the accelerator, releases the clutch and handbrake and shoots towards them. The police then have a real problem. They are obliged to chase a stolen car but also have a duty of care to the people of the area and even to the kid in the car... who is now rushing at them as fast as he can.

The desperate police driver is forced to try to drive up on to the verge where there is a gap in the growing crowd of onlookers. He only just makes it over the kerb before the other car slams into his side, spinning him round. Fortunately his car doesn't hit an onlooker. More people around the crossroads are streaming out to watch. They start cheering as a policeman staggers from his car, he is clearly shaken. The other policeman looks worse as he gets out, his hand going to support his neck as he tries to stand up straight. The RAT driver grins out of his window at the amassing crowds. He waves, they cheer.

The sound of sirens gets closer and he revs his car again. The front bumper is hanging off, the right front wing is smashed in, but the car still looks game. The next police car comes down the bank from Eden Hill, the next estate over, and turns the corner at speed. The driver doesn't get a chance to react before he is hit head on. A huge 'Ooooh' comes from the crowd. Some of them have been forced to run in case the stolen car bounces off the police car and hits them. The RAT reverses at speed but something is loose underneath the car. He rams more and more police cars before he is eventually caught when the engine literally falls out of the car while driving up a bank in the road.

When people go out in the morning they find police cars littered everywhere. A member of the RATS hits every car that comes in to investigate what happened. The police can't even send in tow trucks to get their cars out because kids throw bricks and bottles at them. The police have to walk to the estate from the police station because they have no cars left. On that morning, after the carnage of the night before, the police who normally go out in the patrol cars gather at the station. There is an atmosphere of 'what are we going to do now?' The answer turns out to be that they have to go out and catch a bus to investigate call outs, or use one of the pushbikes they discover in one of the garages. For the residents of The Royal Arms, it was like the news reports of Beirut, cars abandoned and smashed by the side of the road, nervous police hanging around in gangs on the street corners, alert for trouble.

The one driver that started it had personally damaged 14 police cars, six of them totally written off. And then the others joined in. He is later caught and sentenced to five years, an unprecedented time for a child of his age. He was only 13. For Shane as he stands and watches these chases it does something fundamental to his way of thinking. This, he realises, is how you get respect, this is what makes you a star, a local celebrity. This is what he wants to be.

Of course stealing cars is a crime plaguing the country as a whole at this time and occasionally kids from one of the surrounding villages make the mistake of driving a stolen car into Peterlee while on a chase.

The problem is that Peterlee is designed like a rabbit warren. Finding a house by the street number is like taking part in the Krypton Factor quiz show. In every other town and village there seems a logical sequence to the layout: number one is nearly always at the end of town that is closer to the civic buildings. Number one will then be followed by number two. Even if the houses are split into odds on one side of the road and evens on the other, you know where you are. Not so in Peterlee, the big cul-de-sacs often have curved smaller offshoot cul-de-sacs of their own. So number one could be followed by number 48 and then number 69. Drivers who don't know the place get lost as fast as the postmen and delivery drivers.

It is hard to describe Peterlee to people who have never been there before. Yes, it is a post-war new town and an abominable mess created by failures in planning and dodgy construction methods. It suffered under the inept and the corrupt. It is set in between the old colliery villages with their ranks and ranks of two-up and two-down terraced houses with no gardens and cars filling the narrow streets. They shot the movie *Billy Elliot* two miles from Peterlee at Easington colliery. They didn't build film sets; the truth was better than anything they could invent. However at this time the miners' strike is over and the collieries and pits have closed down and unemployment is rising.

Peterlee's natural setting is hardly bettered. It is positioned amid green fields and wooded valleys with an ancient heritage that stretches back long before the Industrial Revolution, into pre-Roman Britain. The east coast of County Durham has large limestone cliffs and sandy beaches. While the villages further inland had pit heaps, here the coal slurry spewed onto the beach.

Today since the closure of the pits, time, tides and weather have largely cleaned these beaches and returned the coast to its original splendid state. Occasionally, though, a coal seam comes close to the seabed underwater, and on a stormy day natural coal dust can wash up, staining the yellow shores with jewel-like black grains, but most times it has vast stretches of clean sands.

The cliffs would often be eroded into valleys by streams flowing down from the higher ground further inland. These wooded valleys are called 'denes' and one of the biggest and best is Castle Eden Dene that reaches deep into the town of Peterlee. It is a wooded nature reserve with 12 miles of wandering pathways passing chasms and waterfalls and wild deer. It eventually leads out on to the beach at Horden, the next village down. The main valley has four large deep tributaries and ravines stretching north into the town, the biggest reaching right into the town centre itself.

The point is that the setting for the town is wonderful. There are open green spaces everywhere and old trees were often left in situ from before the town was built. There are areas of the town on its southern border adjacent to the dene that were later allocated for self-build, Grand Design style developments, so not every estate has its problems. However because these denes cut deep into the town, once you are off the main roads you frequently find yourself on a road to nowhere.

On one such road there is a car chase going on by an 'out of towner'. It leads across Peterlee into such a cul-de-sac at Forth Close. At the bottom of the street, at the dead end of the road, lies North Blunts Infants and Junior School. It is set in the trees at the top of one the main tributary denes leading into the town. The stolen car and the chasing police cars fly down the street but there is no way out. The stolen car bursts through the closed school gates shattering them in an explosion of wooden splinters. It passes the side of the building and finds itself bursting through the yard where all the kids are playing. The playground itself is a Tarmac surface, separated from the drive by a small hedge, but it is about four foot lower than the driveway.

Teachers and children stand horrified as the silver Ford Escort flies off the ground, into the air, and lands in the middle of playtime. The police cars all brake as hard as possible, all desperate to stop before they go into the school grounds. As each car stops, the police, fearing the worst, run to the playground unsure as to what carnage they are about to face. The children have charmed lives, or someone above is looking after them, because not one is hit. The car, though, hasn't finished its madcap journey; it is hurled over the playground, through the fence at the far side, and out into the trees. Twenty foot further on, the thieves in the car get a further shock, the tree line stops suddenly and there is a straight drop down into the bottom of the dene below. The car falls around 30 foot straight down; it hits the ground nose first and stays there without falling over. As the helicopter watches from above, four kids of around 12 years old scramble out of the car, astonishingly unhurt, and run into the thick trees and undergrowth of the nature reserve.

HOUSES

Shane is cheeky, mischievous and cute, but his ginger hair has made him a target for bullies. He is still small for his age and finds himself picked on every day on the estate or at school, on the very rare days he attends.

Even though Dean is his friend, he doesn't always act like it. He is waiting for Shane in Johnson Close near his house.

'Give us a drink of your pop.'

Shane squeezes it tight in his hand, ignoring him. Dean is aggressive, not joking.

'Oi. Are you deaf? I said give us a drink of that.'

'Nah, gerroff.' Shane hugs the bottle close to him.

Dean gets right in his path. His fist shoots out and thumps Shane hard on the end of his nose.

He goes flying back but seems more concerned about his bottle of pop, rather than about where he lands.

Dean looks on amazed, not a drop has been spilt.

Shane gets on his feet and attempts to run around him. Dean sticks his leg out and Shane trips over it. He twists and falls flat on his back; amazingly he still manages to keep the bottle upright. Dean figures Shane should join the circus.

Dean laughs.

'Are you daft? Put the bottle down and fight back.'

'Nah, you're not having it, it's my favourite.'

A kick ends the discussion as the bottle flies out of his hands and smashes in the gutter. Shane shouts,

'Aw, Dean, look what you've done.'

They are still arguing about it when a silver Metro comes by. Behind the wheel are two young teenagers in loud shell suits, and white baseball caps. The hats are pulled down as far as they can go, so that people can't see how young they are.

'Get in.'

It isn't like you might imagine, there isn't a gang, or a number of gangs running the estate, it is simply that there are about 50 or maybe up to 100 kids who live around The Royal Arms who are always getting into trouble. They team up with whomever they meet; they hang around the streets, thieving as a hobby, a way of getting extra money, or even just a way of passing the time. Shane and Dean have moved into a new world since the leisure centre escapade. In only a few weeks they got known as being up for breaking in to houses with older boys. Now they are the first choice for many of the lads who need little kids to shove through small windows.

Shane stares at the Metro from the kerb.

'Where'd you get this from then, its rubbish.'

The lad in the passenger seat is getting out of the two-door car and pulls the seat release forward.

'Get in, man, before the bobbies see us.'

Shane wants to bargain.

'Can we have it when you're finished, take it for a spin?'

'We'll see.'

Dean and Shane get in the back of the car.

Shane discovers that it has rear seat belts; a novelty at this time.

'Do I need to put on my belt?'

There is laughing and various names are thrown around at Shane by the other lads. Shane might be joking, but there again he has seen these lads being chased by the bobbies before.

You can hear the laughter still ringing out as the car revs and pulls away, leaving a cloud of exhaust fumes.

Eventually the car slows as it tours the streets of the estate. They are looking into the back gardens as they drive around. Suddenly the lad in the passenger seat spots what he is looking for.

'There.' He points.

The driver spins the car at the next turn and pulls in. He gets out and walks up the street. He looks around carefully then comes back.

'Can't see anyone there.' He pulls back his seat to let Shane and Dean out. Shane starts to bargain.

'How much?'

Shane stares the driver out.

'How much?'

'A fiver.'

'What? You must be joking. A fiver? Twenty or we walk home now.'

The driver slaps him around the side of his head; it is a ringing blow that brings Shane to the edge of tears. The edge, mind you, but no further, all his friends know he doesn't cry.

'A tenner, and that's it.'

'Aye, okay.' Shane might have agreed but he isn't happy. The driver picks him up, swings him up over the high garden fence, and drops him at the other side. The other boy does the same for Dean. The driver hears Dean shout as he lands on top of Shane.

'Shut up.'

The two older boys get back in the car, start it up and drive around the corner, pulling up outside the short drive up to the front door.

In the back garden, the open window in the downstairs toilet has Shane's feet sticking out, Dean is holding on to them.

Shane's voice is muffled as he hangs upside down in the bathroom.

'I can't find anything to hold on to.'

Dean is unconcerned, 'I'll just drop you, you'll be alright.'

He lets go of Shane's feet which disappear from view, their owner giving a yelp as he lands upside down. It's a good thing that kids don't break easy.

In moments the back door swings open, just as the older two boys come up the side path and into the house.

The driver goes into the front room to find the video player, the passenger runs up the stairs followed by the two young boys.

The passenger goes into the main bedroom, and then pulls the bedding off the bed. While he is doing that, the two young lads are going through the table tops and drawers.

'...Only if it looks gold, don't take anything else, the bobbies will spot it; gold gets melted straight down.'

The older boy has taken the pillowcases off the pillows and gives a whistle as he drops them down the staircase.

'Do ya need the quilt?'

The shout comes back. 'Aye, think so.'

He drops it down after the pillowcases. Shane and Dean have found rings, bracelets and chains. They all drop their finds into the remaining pillowcase, then the lad moves off back downstairs. It is all happening so fast they must have only been in the house for two minutes. In the bedroom Dean grabs his stomach and doubles up.

'Shane, I need a poo.'

'Well, have one then.'

Dean grins then jumps on the bed drops his trousers and squats.

Immediately Dean gives a loud fart and the smell hits the room at 100mph.

'Argh, that's horrible.'

Dean has dumped a huge brown steaming turd on the bed and then wipes his bum on the pillows.

Shane is open mouthed. 'What did you do that for?'

'I dunno, I just wanted to do it.'

The stench is making Shane's eyes water as Dean pulls up his trousers. It seems worse than anything Shane has smelt before.

'Argh, that's manky that.'

The older boy runs back into the room.

'Right, out of here now.'

He sees the turd sitting on the white sheet and brown-stained pillow beside it.

'You dirty git, you're not right in the head you.'

Shane and Dean giggle and run off downstairs.

For the record, this modus operandi becomes Dean's trademark at nearly every house he burgles. When eventually DNA testing comes into use, the police have cast-iron evidence of Dean's crimes. Find a turd at the scene of a break in? Then go out, arrest Dean and stick him in the cell until the DNA test comes back. They don't even need to search the database; they just keep a laminated copy of Dean's print-out results to compare them to.

When Shane and Dean get in the living room they can see that the video player is in a pillowcase, and the huge Technics hi-fi system is in the quilt cover taken from the bed.

'Okay, we're out.'

Everything is picked up and straight out the door. The car engine is still running. They don't bother with the boot, it's too small. The gear goes on the floor in the rear as the lads jump in and move off.

It's only as they pull away they see a teenager coming out of a house further down the street. He stands, his face a picture when he sees them. He doesn't live there; he is the lookout while his mates are busy robbing.

Shane's car drives off beeping the horn to alert the neighbours. Laughing, they scoot off leaving the other thieves to it.

Six streets away they stop.

The driver turns to Shane.

'You're on the knock.'

Shane gets out and walks up to a house and rings the doorbell. It has a new aluminium door and window frames, clearly it belongs to someone who has bought his council house or, as they say on the estate, someone posh.

Eventually it opens and a man answers holding a slice of toast in his hand. He is dressed smartly with a shirt and a tie. It looks like he has just returned from work. He looks down at Shane.

'Mister, do want to buy a video player? My mam can't find the rent this month and she says I have to sell it.'

His face drops, his little lips quiver and his eyes fill up with tears.

'It was my birthday present an' all.'

The man looks down and seems about to close the door before he relents.

'How much?'

'She has to have a hundred and twenty pounds for it, it's top of the range, brand new.'

The man thinks hard.

'A hundred pounds.'

'No, sorry, has to be a hundred and twenty, it's a new Sony, it's worth it.'

'Where is it?'

'I'll get it now if you want.'

He disappears around the corner back to the car. Shane is handed it, he says to the boys, 'Ninety pounds, is that alright?'

'No, they go for a ton.'

Shane stands there.

'I know but he won't pay.'

The lure of a fast turnover wins through.

'Aye, go on then.'

Shane takes the video player and runs off as fast

he can, disappearing around the corner. The driver sighs.

'He's a fly little bairn that one.'

The other lad agrees.

'I bet he tries to sell him the Technics.'

At the house Shane hands over the video and holds out his hand.

'A hundred and twenty, Mister.'

The man disappears back inside and comes back with a roll of notes. He pays out a hundred and ten pounds.

'That's it, take it or leave it.'

Shane takes it and pauses.

'A mate of mine is selling a six hundred pound Technics hi-fi, he only wants a hundred and fifty for that, interested?'

The man strokes his chin.

'It's not nicked, is it?'

Shane: 'No, Mister, I promise.'

He counts out another hundred and fifty as he looks down at Shane. Shane grins back.

*

It's an hour later on the side road leading to the local sports field. The two older boys are walking away with the bulk of the money in their pockets, the jewellery and other stuff from the house is split between a pair of sports bags. On the footie pitch a group of kids are kicking a ball at the goal. Dean has gone home too and little Glen, a lad from around the corner, has arrived. He is standing looking at Shane who is still inside the silver Metro

He is trying to sit in the front of the car, but cannot see over the top of the dashboard so is standing with his bum perched on the edge of the seat.

Glen isn't convinced that Shane can manage.

'What about the pedals?'

He presses on the accelerator and the engine roars.

Glen jumps in and slams the door.

Shane manages to get his other foot on the clutch and bangs it into gear. The car shoots away down the road. The engine screams as the car moves, over-revving because it is still in first gear.

Shane can't grip the wheel properly; it feels alive in his hand. The car hits the kerb and then spins on to the grass.

The football players run for their lives as the car careens about. It spins, then shoots forward straight towards the goal mouth. In Shane's head he can see clearly what he wants to do. He imagines driving the car across the faded white line. 'Goal!' He imagines a crowd cheering wildly as the car gets tangled in the net.

Of course in reality it misses the goal completely and heads towards the tree line. After trying to spin the car round and round in circles, it ploughs up furrows in the field and then stalls.

In the time-honoured fashion of joyriders everywhere in Britain, they use a cigarette lighter to set fire to some paper then torch the car and leave it burning. As adults come out the houses towards them, the lads run away in the opposite direction, late for their teas.

LOST

John Canning is just putting the kettle on and making a tuna fish sandwich when the doorbell rings. His wife is due back soon from the shops, so he's making her favourite too: marmite toast, though how she likes such a foul concoction he hasn't a clue. The doorbell rings again and he wonders who it might be.

He opens the door and at first sees nobody there; until his eyes drop down to see two angelic looking young faces staring up at him.

'Mister, can you tell us where Peterlee is? We're lost.'

They stand with earnest, innocent faces, and his heart goes out to them.

'Peterlee?'

He sounds alarmed, 'That's miles away, this is Durham.'

'I'm hungry, Mister, can we have a biscuit? Please.'

'Oh, of course come in.'

They are shown into the living room. Canning is flustered as he realises just how difficult this is, and just how dodgy this might look to someone outside.

What if someone comes in and misinterprets what is going on. He is alone with two small children; he is suddenly desperate for the return of his wife. He knows the first thing he must do is to ring the police. 'Right now,' he thinks. 'To put down a marker' and 'keep everything above board'.

'What's your name, son?' he asks Shane.

'Billy, what's yours, Mister?'

'I'm Mr Canning, and what's your name?' Turning to Taz.

'Tommy, Sir.'

'What lovely polite boys you are.'

Together: 'Thank you, Mister.'

He is charmed.

'I just need to call the police and let them know where you are.'

'Can we have a drink first please. If it's not too much trouble.'

'Oh yes, of course, what would you like?'

'Do you have any milk please?'

'I'm sure I can find some.'

He leaves the room and instantly the two children spring into action. The first thing they look for are any handbags, they nearly always have money in them. Shane is opening drawers, fast but very quietly. Taz has closed the room door silently and put his body weight against it to get a warning of Canning's return.

Shane hasn't found anything yet and is getting

frustrated. They have been away from home for four days now. This is their preferred way of making money. Although they are only nine years old they have come to understand the importance of the getaway. They pay for a driver and the car out of their takings.

Their driver, Jon, is waiting half a street away. He is 14 but looks older. The car is a white Nova, legal, inasmuch as it is 'bought' in the name of Jon's father, and not stolen, though obviously it's not insured. It is a rust bucket, but has one great advantage; because Jon's faked his father's signature on the log book, it's not registered as missing and therefore not of interest to the police. Such were the days before computers and the way things are regulated now.

The boys do four or five jobs a day; their record and personal best is ten such burglaries, and Jon gets an equal share, usually anywhere between £200 and £3,000 a day. He isn't greedy; it's good money and has no risks. If the kids are being chased or caught, he ignores them; there's nothing the police can do to them, they are too young.

If they make it out of the house without anyone coming after them they get in the car unseen, drive off and do another job a mile or so away. Their last event of the day has become a ritual; after their last job, they go shopping to buy more expensive trainers and shell suits than they can possibly wear, together with piles of food, sweets and drink. Yesterday the kids bought sleeping bags and stored them in the boot. He pulled the car into his dad's garage for the night and the kids feasted and slept in the car 'til morning when it all started again.

Jon is pulled from his daydreams as he sees a woman approach the house where the boys are. Shane hears the front door open and jumps on to the sofa, Taz slinks away from the door, which bursts open.

'Oh, who are you?'

She is middle aged and dressed like a granny with a coat, skirt and blouse. She peers over her glasses at them.

Canning comes through with two glasses of milk.

'Ah, you've met our little guests, they're lost.'

He looks down on them with affection.

'The poor wee lambs are so far away from home in Peterlee.'

His wife is more suspicious and savvy; she is clearly confused about how they could have got here by themselves, so many miles away from home. He jumps in, on their side almost protectively, but she seems to have a heart of stone.

'Look darling, I think it's for the best if we let the police know where they are, their mums and dads must be worried sick.'

He leaves the room. They turn their innocent little faces on her.

'Missus, he said we could have a biscuit.'

'Yes, we are really hungry.'

Taz looks ready to burst into tears. Whatever

suspicions she has, she softens and reacts immediately.

'Of course, you little poppets.'

She leaves the room.

Taz has already spotted that she has put down her handbag on a chair and his hand is inside removing her purse in split seconds. Shane looks around fast; the only thing he hasn't already checked out is a biscuit tin in the corner of the room, on top of a piano stool. He grabs it mainly because he is hungry. He holds it tight under his arms and they are off.

They dash into the hall straight past Canning as he is trying, not very successfully, to explain to the police that two lost and tiny children are in his house.

It only takes a second's pause for it to be too late. Canning is doing his best with the police control room.

'Yes, very young, they looked scared and lost.'

He looks bewildered as they run out of the front door.

Outside the car is already slowly moving towards the house as they get to the garden gate.

Canning is caught between going after them and being rude to the police mid-sentence.

'Where are you going? No, sorry not you... No it's the children, they've run out the house.'

If he was to put the phone down immediately and chase after them they could be caught, but he is polite and it seems wrong to stop his conversation while talking to the police, so he shouts out for his wife.

'Darling, can you see to the... No sorry, not you, sorry DARLING, the kids...'

By the time she looks out of the door they are around the corner. Jon has already driven alongside and picked them up. As he drives away they lie on the floor in the back. Shane opens the tin; to his astonishment it doesn't have biscuits in it, it is packed with rolls and rolls of cash. Shane rocks back with a scream of delight and pulls off the elastic bands that hold the bundles together. He starts to whoop and throw the money in the air. Taz screams out a massive shout and the driver can't believe his eyes through the mirror. The car speeds off, if anyone had been following they would have seen what £6,000 looks like when it is being thrown in the air by two wild and happy nine year olds about to have the biggest spending spree of their life.

As the jobs roll on and they get more and more money, they prove that even little thieves can fall out. Sometimes a roll of cash gets slipped down into their underpants and they try to hold back from their partners in crime. So, as if they know the life that lies ahead, they develop a routine of conducting strip searches on each other, just to make sure they are not being ripped off.

INTERVENTION

Though Shane and Taz are enjoying themselves no one else seems to be. Jon finds that the Nova is a faster car than he had allowed for and smashes it and himself into a brick wall. The young lads aren't bothered, they have no real idea about money and don't understand the impact they have on other people's lives. They know they can go out and score and get some more money, so it doesn't really matter. It's just a daily thing, it's what they do every day. They don't care. They literally have no morals, it doesn't matter if those they stole from were young or old anyhow. At nine everyone is old, they just burgle from whoever they come across. They are totally naive, ruthless, opportunist thieves.

Taz, Dean and Shane run away from home because their mothers won't let them go out to play or knock around together. So they escape every chance they get. The police are constantly out hunting for them, while Maz and Dean's mum worry at home. It will be four or five days out, constant grafting, constant burgling, and constantly pinching cars.

Well, in fairness, the only cars that Shane and Dean can pinch themselves, unless they get older lads to do it for them, are Austin Metros. They have the weakest of all steering locks and Shane and Dean can break them if they hang on to it together, pulling down hard with their combined weight.

When they do get in the car there are other problems, like seeing over the top of the dashboard, so they go equipped with cushions to lift them up high enough. It must be bad enough to have kids steal your car but can you imagine what it was like watching a car drive down the road driven by small nine year olds who are too short to see where they are going, too weak to turn the wheel and control the car, never mind having zero level of understanding about the rules of the road? How Shane, Dean and Taz survive their childhood years is a miracle in itself, but Shane comes to learn that he is mistaken if he thinks he is too young to escape any consequences.

Maz tries to stop his pocket money, but it does no good. He earns far more than she gets in benefits, never mind how much he gets from her.

She says to her neighbours she doesn't believe in hitting children apart from a smack on his hand but then Shane just looks at her and says, 'It doesn't hurt anyway.' She takes his things from him, but it doesn't do any good. He smashes things up in his bedroom and she relents to keep him quiet. Given the scale of what is happening, it's easy for her to end up saying, 'What's the point 'cos it's not working?'

She tells a friend as they sit having a pint in The Royal Arms,

'I've tried to punish him by giving him no sweets or luxuries, like cakes and biscuits. He's terrible for his biscuits and cakes, is our Shane. But he sneaks in to the fridge in the kitchen, gets them himself, and takes them upstairs anyway. So no matter what I've done with him, it doesn't work. Shane is Shane. If he gets something in his head, he will do what he wants to do. Nobody can stop him.'

Social services now have a file on him so thick they need a wheelbarrow, and he gives the police so much extra work they should have had an increase in their budget; Shane is a nightmare. But there again the whole family have become something of a legend.

Maz has a philosophy when it came to raising Shane:

'If anybody comes to the door and complains about him, I take no notice. If I'd seen it for myself, then yes, I will punish him. But if somebody comes up to my door, complaining about him, I'll say, "I haven't seen him do it, so I can't check him for it". I'm not taking anyone's word for anything; you need proof, don't you? You know, innocent until proven guilty.'

Many of the neighbours on the estate think Shane is funny. 'Just imagine tiny kids pinching cars, and he looks as if butter wouldn't melt in his mouth!'

They talk about it in The Royal Arms and chat about it in the shops.

Maz is watching the telly with her feet up when there is a knock at the door. Another knock, again and again; a loud voice shouts 'Maz.'

When she gets to the door her neighbour is pointing up the street.

'Maz! There's a man's got Shane in the house, he's blaming him for trying to pinch the car.'

Maz runs around fast, following her neighbour up the street, who gets to the open door of a house and points; she's out of breath. Maz runs straight in, barging past the woman who lives there. A man is holding Shane down on the floor, kneeling, straddling him, as he pins him down. Shane is in a fury, trying to punch, kick, or bite out at the man holding him. The woman catches up with Maz and grabs her saying,

'We've called the police, we caught him trying to steal our Metro.'

It is a bad idea to try to grab Maz; she punches the woman with a clubbing right fist. Shane to this very day is extremely defensive about his mum, and swears down blind that she never punched the woman.

Maz shouts, 'He wouldn't try and steal your car, he's a good little boy.'

The woman staggers over backwards and hits the wall.

Maz then grabs the man by his hair, screaming, 'I'll kill you,' and hauls him off backwards. The woman she hit slides down the wall legs wide apart, into sitting position on the floor. Her nose is bleeding.

Maz hasn't let go of the man's hair and, as he fails to get up off the floor, she is kicking him in his ribs, then, still holding his hair up in her left hand, she starts to hit him around the head with her right fist.

Shane now is off the floor and joins in until the man lies passed out on the floor.

'Come on, darling.' She grabs Shane's little hand and they walk back home together. Her neighbour eyes up the carnage inside the house, mentally recording the full details, ready to entertain the pub crowd later on about yet another of Maz's exploits. The police sirens are sounding in the distance and getting louder.

'You didn't pinch the car, did you, Shane?' she asks as she replays in her mind what has just happened with an increased sense of nervousness.

'No, mam, I wouldn't do anything like that.'

'Good boy.'

That night as the pints flow in the pub, a version of what happened gets more and more gruesome with every telling, as it spreads around the tables.

Maz confides in her neighbour:

'I shouldn't have done it, I believed Shane, but it turns out it is true, little monster, he did try to nick it.'

She gives a sigh.

'I've had more fights than enough over him. But you have to, haven't you? He's my son. He's my life, isn't he?'

Her neighbour is quick to agree with Maz. It pays to in the long run, besides there are those who would kill for a ringside seat like hers.

Things only become worse when another powerful role model moves into his house. When Shane is nine, Robert, his mam's stepbrother, moves in with Gordon, Maz and Shane. Why he lost his home is probably easy to guess. Robert is trouble; he is a fighter, a drunk and has a drug habit. He is in and out of prison and it's a fact that many prisoners lose their houses when they face a long stretch, many too lose them because of drug habits.

Shane sees him as his hero. He is still being bullied for trivial reasons, some boys picking on him because he's ginger, others because he always has money and they want it off him. Robert takes the boy under his wing and takes pleasure in the young lad's adoration. Shane finds that when he walks in the street beside Robert, striding out and in step within the shadow of his hero, no one bothers him.

Robert, especially when drunk, commands that strange term called 'respect' from others. What that really means of course, is fear, alienation, and being fawned over by people who are scared of you. Robert was the father figure that Shane adopted. He could do no wrong in his eyes; and everything that Robert did was to be emulated.

The problem is that Robert is in and out of prison, one minute he's there to protect and guide Shane, the next he's locked up and Shane is fair game for the older kids.

The weeks have passed and Robert is back in prison.

Another neighbour wakes to a noise. She waits, her body lying still, listening in case someone is in the house. Eventually she tires of waiting and, like many others who don't want disturbing truths in the middle of the night, shrugs and goes back to sleep. In the morning she goes into her garden only to find a car wedged between the two walls of the alley between her house and the one next door.

The car is upside down, three foot off the ground and wedged absolutely tight. People come from all streets around the estate to see it before the fire brigade arrives and is forced to cut it apart. No one can figure out how the kids that nicked it got out of it, the doors are wedged shut, the windows intact and fully up. No doubt, someone in The Royal Arms suggests, it was caught in a levitation beam by aliens in a UFO. Shane and Taz know the truth, because they wriggled out through the drop-down armrest set into the rear seats and then out through the boot which they then closed after them.

The neighbours might be impressed at the real-life soap drama in their midst but social services are not. They are putting a care plan into effect; curfews and home-based restrictions don't work: Shane is to be put into care.

The social worker is nervous as she sits on the sofa in Maz's house, even though a policeman accompanies her. In truth, he too is a bit nervous, and jokes to himself that it might have been better to have a tactical response team on standby, or at least to have worn his stab vest. A cleverer policeman, however, wouldn't be joking about it to himself, he would have made sure to wear the vest before going on the visit. The social worker is trying to explain.

'Yes, Maz, the age of criminal responsibility has always been ten years of age so anybody committing crimes under the age of ten will not face the criminal justice system, and will not hit the criminal court. But we do have alternative actions to be taken in response to law breaking by children. Those who regularly break the law can be taken into care.'

'You'll get him out of here over my dead body.'

Shane is cuddling into his mother and is just beginning to understand what this all about.

'Mam, don't let them take me away.' He is holding on to her for grim death.

'Maz, I have the order here, please don't make it worse than it is.'

She waves it in front of her.

Maz grabs the paper out of her hand and, before the social worker can react, tears it in half and throws it on the fire. It burns instantly.

'You can't do that…'

Maz stands, looming over the stricken social worker.

'I can't do what?'

The social worker has gone white and the policeman moves over quickly to her side.

'Maz, stop that.'

'Stop what? And my name is Mrs Taylor not bloody Maz, you don't get to call me that.'

'Mrs Taylor then, please sit down or I'll arrest you

for threatening behaviour.'

Maz shouts, 'You can't take him without a court order, show me it.'

The social worker acts bewildered.

'You've just torn it up and thrown it on the fire.'

'No I haven't, prove it.'

The social worker emboldened by the presence of the policeman gleefully produces her masterstroke, and whips out another piece of paper.

'Hah, they told me you'd do this, so I have a second copy, see…'

Her hands fly up to her face as her nose is squashed back into her face.

'You're not taking Shane.'

The policeman piles in, but he's young and in his worst nightmares he never imagines being assaulted by a mother and her nine year old. When his inspector arrives later, he shakes his head as he tears a strip off the duty sergeant on his radio.

'You let someone just out of probation come here by themselves with just a social worker? At Maz Taylor's house? Unbelievable.'

Maz is arrested for assault, it will take hours before she is cautioned and let out. Shane can be seen lying down in the back seat of the social worker's car, trying to break the windows with his feet while a policeman is trying to hold him down. The social worker's nose has stopped bleeding but she's going to have two black eyes in the morning.

The law is quite simple, if somebody under the age of ten commits regular crimes of any sort they are dealt with by social services. There has to be some intervention some involving of agencies like education, the police, even possibly the probation service, to try and prevent further offending.

The emphasis in youth justice is always on prevention rather than punishment; the whole aim is to correct re-offending as soon as possible. However Shane seems to lie outside every strategy, tactic, and action plan and, although nobody will admit it, everyone seems to be waiting until he is ten in order to find some meaningful answers.

Children's homes are expensive, a placement might cost £4,000 a week, a problematic placement that needs special 'one-to-one' support might mean double or even treble that. The costs are eye watering. It is also worth looking carefully at the way in which the system works. Children's homes are the places where you put the most vulnerable, at risk children, to protect them. For example, children whose parents have died and have no other relatives, or children who have been beaten and abused, these are all put in children's homes as a place of safety, with a sympathetic and caring support team around them. These, however, are also where you put the worst offending kids.

So what do you think happens?

In the past there have been cases where a very

young teenager who was a sexual predator was placed in a home along with vulnerable previously sexually exploited children. There are no prizes for guessing the outcome. In Middlesbrough there was a case of all the little innocent kids being pimped out down the bus station by older kids who had a history of abuse and abusing.

It is a system that is deeply flawed; at times it leaves you speechless.

*

For Shane; he is being driven off to his first placement in a children's home, while his mam is being cautioned down the police station. Even before Maz gets released, Shane has already run away from the home after starting a fire and causing devastation. He then goes missing for five days before turning up back at his mam's house again.

This becomes a year of a constant cycle of interventions, foster homes, spells back with Maz and curfew orders. Placements in children's homes often result in Shane being at the heart of burglaries being committed by him and other mini offenders. With his help, bravado and know how, they break into houses, steal cars, and are able to ignore the police because they are under ten. He doesn't really organise other kids, he doesn't form gangs, but he is so up for trouble, so unconcerned about what he does, that he seems to be a catalyst for others to copy and emulate his actions. When he gets fed up, he runs away and ends up back home; the kids he leaves behind carry out a sub-franchise crime wave of their own.

*

So what does it means in practice for someone like Shane, what are the costs we face as a society? Do the maths, think it through. If we take a low average: four or five burglaries a day, then add car theft, malicious damage and arson. From when Shane started his life of crime at six to ten years old he probably committed five crimes a day, that's 35 a week, 1,820 a year, an estimated 7,280 in these four years.

These statistics are primarily felt by one police station resourced to deal with crime in a town of 30,000. Each one of those crime statistics represents pain and trouble to the people of Peterlee. It is difficult to find the real figures but if the average cost of a stolen car back then was only £1,000 (they tended to be older cars), and nearly every one of them was either set on fire after the joyride or written off in crashes. Then the average burglary was worth say £500. We can't even guess at the cost of fires; it's usually the cars that are set on fire, but sometimes it's garages, sheds, empty houses or shops. Let us leave aside the personal cost to people who lose family heirlooms and prize possessions, the bottom line is that Shane must have cost the people of the town and the insurance companies around £7.3 million. It is worth repeating this figure. One child aged between six and ten, in one small town of 30,000 people in the North East of England, caused mayhem to the estimated sum of £7.3 million, maybe much more, in a four-year period.

Now add the costs to the state of £200,000 per annum in specialist childcare costs and then the wages of social workers, the fire brigade, and the police.

Then, of course, the sobering thought, we remember there are plenty of other Shanes out there.

*

Birthdays are usually celebrated events, but most come and go without any real impact; one day really is much the same as another. At one simple sweep of the second hand on the clock, it moves at midnight from one day and one date to another. It is now 12th December 1990. Shane is suddenly ten years old and his world changes, he has crossed the line of the age of criminal responsibility. Now Shane will be dealt with by the full powers of the state, including the deprivation of his liberty. Now he can be placed in a children's secure unit, iron bars, high security fences, locked doors and staff that won't be intimidated.

For anybody appearing in the court over the age of ten, the magistrates have sentencing guidelines. So when someone first appears in the court they start at the lower end of the options available to them.

This is how magistrates choose from their list of

options. It starts like this: referral orders to the youth justice team and the young offender multi-agency team. Here children have to attend appointments, a contract is drawn up with them about their behaviour. If that doesn't work, they move on to more intervention with social services, probation, then intensive supervision. From there they move on to an attendance centre where they've got to go for a certain number of hours, and then they gradually work up the scale to detention and training orders, which is effectively custody in a specialist institution for young people up to the age of 17. Finally, once everything else has been tried, there are low length custodial sentences, up to higher lengths, depending on the severity of the crime. Associated with that is a period on release where the young offenders are again intensively monitored and where an element of training is given, trying to use their time constructively, aiming again at prevention of re-offending behaviour.

*

This is his first arrest of this era; the charges are burglary and car theft. Shane is ten and looks innocent and stands in court with his mam. The clerk says,

'Court rise.'

Maz know the score, she stands and Shane, watching carefully, follows her to his feet. The magistrates file into the court, three of them. Two men, one woman. They all are old, wear glasses and talk in ways that

Shane has only ever seen on telly. The magistrates have heard all the horror stories before they come into the courtroom from their antechamber. This is where they take tea and look at who is going to be up before them on the day. They are fair and take seriously that everything he has done previously was when he was below the age of responsibility and therefore outside their active interest in this matter. The first thing they do is to refer Shane to the young offender team.

Shane walks outside the court with his mam; it is the first of what is to come, weekly, often three times a week, of being brought up on fresh charges. Some days in court they are charging him with 20 new offences. Before the first sentence and intervention can be organised with the young offender team, his list of new offences is swamping the system.

ELEMORE

Andy Smith is nervous; he doesn't like interviews but really wants the job. It is the post of residential childcare welfare officer at Elemore Hall. Elemore is a busy Durham County Council special school for pupils who have social, emotional and mental health difficulties.

The drive to Elemore Hall is beautiful. It turns off from Easington Lane, an old colliery pit village with poor terraced cottages, up a few hundred yards from there and on to Hetton on the Hill. This ancient agricultural hamlet seems a thousand miles away from the village it leaves behind; then over the hill to a turn into a private drive.

Andy motors down the beautiful tree-lined path, rehearsing all the imagined questions he is likely to be asked. The hall comes into view in the floor of the valley. All around are wooded hills cutting it off completely from its surroundings. It is a fabulous location, an old 18th century manor house with added modern buildings set in extensive grounds in the open countryside. It has been a school since 1958 and sits in the middle of 40 acres of woods and farmland. Elemore has 86 pupils over the age of 12 who have found it difficult to achieve success in mainstream education. There are 25 residents and 61 extended day pupils.

Andy has studied Elemore's mission statement and its vision to 'create a happy, positive, successful and worthwhile place to be for all members of the school community'. He can work with that, after all by nature he is a happy man and believes in the ethos of the school. He is well aware that all of the young people are likely to be damaged in one way or another and have come with a lot of baggage.

'To see every single child as an individual,' he thinks, 'a unique individual; there's always a way in and you then build up rapport and respect for each and everyone you are dealing with.'

In working with young people he knows that sometimes you must give them some form of responsibility and get them to thrive on a position of trust. Some will relish little charts to see the progress they are making, some respond to praise and others have a sense of humour and just need to have a bit of a crack and carry on. Everybody is different but there is always some way in.

He confidently parks the car and makes his way up the steps to the front entrance. The receptionist sits behind a glass screen that looks more like a post office security window than a normal school. It looks very well protected. The school motto is emblazoned on a sign above the desk, it says, 'Together Everyone Achieves More'.

Andy tells the receptionist that he is here for the interview and is told in turn to grab a seat. A short young boy with ginger hair stops amid the melee of kids and tired frazzled teachers coming in and out of the hallway.

Andy's hair is thinning and he nervously pats it down and checks his side parting is still in place. The kid is staring and he feels that something is wrong. He unobtrusively does that nervous check run down: hair OK, tie straight, a quick glance to make sure his flies aren't undone; and then sits back, he is alright. His sister had actually sent off for the details of the job and he only filled in the application to keep her happy.

Now he realises he really wants the position, despite the kid with the ginger hair, ten feet away, staring at him and giving him the evil eye. Andy gives a pleasant friendly smile. The boy's face doesn't respond in any way, in fact his eyes seem to harden. Andy knows that all the kids here are disturbed and wonders what his story is.

The headteacher, Mike Daley, comes out of his office at a door just off reception and introduces himself.

'Hi, I'm Mike, you must be Andy.'

'Yes, that's right, Andy Smith, thank you for seeing me.'

He glances around, the ginger-haired boy has disappeared. 'Scared of the headteacher,' he thinks.

'Come on through.'

They go into a small committee-type of room, there are just the two of them, though the receptionist pops her head around the door and offers Andy a coffee.

He is grateful. It is always something to do, isn't it? It's always good to have things in your hands, stops you waggling them about. The small talk phase passes well, the coffee isn't too hot and if there are any awkward questions he can always take a sip and stall while thinking of the answers.

'Tell me, Andy, why do you want this job?'

The 200-year-old room is a mix of the old panelled walls and flickering, institutional, fluorescent strip lighting above. As Andy is about to answer, something catches his eye. He glances out of the window at the wonderful views of the valley and nearly spills his coffee on to his suit trousers. The ginger kid is standing outside on the window ledge and looking in. As the principal and Andy turn, he gives them a huge grin. He starts banging on the window and shouts through.

'Who's he, Mike?'

The headteacher covers his pained expression and replies calmly,

'Not now, Shane, I'm busy I've go a job interview with this young man here.'

Shane isn't satisfied with the answer.

'What's his name, Mike? Is he gonna work here? Do you think he'll last long?'

Andy is aware of the scrutiny as the kid passes judgement and doesn't wait for the headteacher's answer.

'Nah, he won't last long.'

Mr Fellows loves using history to try to engage with his pupils. He is trying a Horrible History approach. Tales of murder, rape, pillage and plunder, 'If that doesn't interest the little beggars then nothing will.'

The classroom overlooks the car park at the side of the hall. The classroom should be full but there are some notable absences,

'Shane isn't here,' he notices, 'that means it's straight to see the head after this.'

Shane has been sent to the 'school of last resort' and spends Monday to Friday here as a boarder but goes home at weekends. However since it isn't a secure institution he can walk out with nothing to stop him. Fellows has mixed feelings about Shane; he wants to be part of the team that changes his life around, but that is tempered by the fact that Shane and one of his friends, it transpires, were the little shits who stole his car a year ago. It's hard to want to help and be resentful at the same time. He is still on the fence.

He launches into the lesson.

'This area was first inhabited around four thousand years ago, there were Bronze Age cities, towns and villages here before the Romans came, before the Emperor Hadrian built his wall to keep out the Scots. Over the centuries Durham stood strong and when the Vikings landed on its coast in 960 AD and burned to the ground the ancient village of Yoden which lies under the fields of Peterlee...'

He knows that Shane is from Peterlee; he put that in on purpose to see if it would provoke some form of interest. Shame he's not here.

He is starting to hit his stride, he needs to, the kids are all slouching in their chairs, and one looks asleep. He puts more effort and enthusiasm into his voice.

'It thrived under the Norman invasion and achieved unrivalled power in the country. In those days the Bishop of Durham had the powers of a prince: he had his own parliament, his own army and could mint his own coins. He built the harbour at Hartlepool five miles south of modern Peterlee. It was from here that King John ordered the building of the city walls over the harbour, and the treasure ship that sailed with the ransom for Richard the Lionheart set out to sea from here.'

The kids look more alert, one nudges the next. Mr Fellows feels a touch of pride welling up; it's working, he is getting to them.

'The area saw great bloodshed when the real life "Braveheart" William Wallace brought his Scottish armies marching through the fields here in 1305 on his way to York. A few years later, in 1346, the Scots were defeated just outside Durham at Neville's Cross...'

He drops his voice into what he hopes is an engaging hush, his voice dark and husky, as if doing a voice over for a horror film. He feels that his past amateur dramatic work is paying off.

'...but the biggest killer of all was still to come. During the first half of 1349 the Black Death plague came into the country and spread northwards.'

The children are smiling and there is a feeling of excitement in the room. 'It's the plague that does it,' he decides. 'What is it about mass death that so gets to kids?'

'In May it reached York, and during the summer months of June, July and August, it ravaged the North. Within five hundred days it crossed the entire country. The numbers killed have been estimated as being as high as two million dead.'

He pauses for effect, the kids are all now sitting straight, everyone looking at him, all of them smiling.

Behind and unbeknown to him, Shane is looking through into the classroom. He is making a shush sign, finger to his lips, then makes a rude sign indicating what he thinks of the lesson. The children inside the classroom are struggling not to laugh.

Mr Fellows prepares himself. Here is the hard part, giving some relevance to the past, bringing it up to their own lives, to let them see how things connect. He launches into the point of his lesson.

'The area was decimated and only revived when the Industrial Revolution came to the North in the eighteen thirties. Miners came in great numbers from Wales and Cornwall as the minefields opened and coal became the new "King of the North" and stayed that way until the nineteen seventies.'

Shane is holding up ten fingers to the window, nine… eight… seven…

'Practically every village around the city had a coal

mine, only the city itself remained free of industries. Villages with only a hundred inhabitants changed within ten years to eight thousand people or more crammed into tiny terraced houses right next to the pitheads where the shafts dropped down below ground into the pit.'

Two… one… The hand withdraws quickly and disappears.

Suddenly the windows thunder as sticks and stones are hurled from the car park. Fellows runs to the window only to have it break as he tries to look out.

'Arrgh!' A shard of glass nicks his cheek.

Shane has managed to attract a gang around him to join in and they are breaking all the windows on the ground floor. They stand laughing outside flashing V-signs to the staff. The kids inside whoop with joy. The shouts of the teachers sound out as they run along the corridors to chase the teenage marauders away. Maybe Viking genes have survived and risen again to the surface as the kids practise their pillaging skills.

*

The days turn into weeks and the weeks into months.

Andy Smith is running full pelt trying to catch up with Shane. Whatever else he can do, the kid can't run for toffee. They race through the woods and

Andy knows he will catch him in a moment, that is until a branch snaps back and hits him in the face. He staggers for a second, and then he puts on a spurt and is quickly within a hair's breadth of the boy. He extends his leading foot and kicks the heel of Shane, who now teeters forward, arms flailing as he runs and eventually falls into a roll and lands face down in a heap. Andy drops on top of him and shouts for the others. Their voices can be heard in the trees behind them.

Shane is pinned to the ground. It must hurt because Andy's knee is digging into his back but he doesn't cry out, he just wiggles to ease the pressure. Andy rolls him on to his back. Shane's face is a picture of hate.

*

In the few months since Andy has taken up his post Shane has been a nightmare. All of the ideas Andy had about wooing kids over into a better frame of mind have failed with Shane. In the first days of his residency Shane persuaded another boy, a year older, to run off with him. They escaped into the woods and made their way into the village nearby. They stole around £5,000 from a pizza shop and acquired a Nissan Bluebird, which led to a police chase involving traffic cars and helicopters. By the time they got to Middlesbrough, Shane now aged 12, the other boy 13, had travelled for miles on the wrong side of a dual carriageway heading directly into the oncoming traffic. Police cars sealed off the junction, Shane tried to turn off and he was forced to go up an embankment at high speed. There was an almighty bang, the car smashed through a fence, bumped into a field, stalled and then kept rolling on, bouncing up and down over the ploughed mud. The other lad jumped out of the car and got away.

The police usually focus primarily on the driver not the passenger, and so Shane was caught and given a sharp slap or two by the police. It is easy to criticise them but they knew only too well just how much danger he had been to the public and other drivers. Their hearts were beating hard, adrenaline pumping, as they had been forced to follow him against the traffic. He was dragged across the field, and handcuffed to a lamppost until a big police van arrived to take him away. He was returned to Elemore Hall. No other punishment was on offer.

*

Andy is panting hard as the other teachers come through the trees.

Andy looks up.

'How is he?'

'Touch and go, they hope he'll make it.'

The boy that has been beaten up is receiving treatment from the paramedics and ambulance team. He is an older boy, bigger, stronger. It was known that he was a bully who was picking on Shane and others of the boys. Shane is still small for his age and is an enigma. He is picked on and bullied but never beaten down; he is resilient and always bounces back. He is the naughtiest kid in the school. He still isn't a gang leader, but other kids flock around him nevertheless. He is an influence, he does something and others automatically join in.

Shane had decided to leave the school to go on a jaunt and once he announced it others wanted to come along for the ride. The strange thing is that the older boy clearly saw something in what was going on and wanted to be part of it, despite the fact that they were younger kids who he picked on.

The boy is 17 years old, five years older than them, yet here he is following them as they walk off over the grass. The ground falls away down a dip; away from prying eyes, and then goes further down into a small shallow lake. The small boys are nervous of the older boy who is following them.

How it starts is hard to say. Was it something said? A look? A threat?

One moment it is a bunch of young kids being stalked by an older boy. The next the dynamic has changed. They look at the boy with hard, hateful eyes. Before he can pick up on the new reality they run and are on him. He goes to take a backward step but can't and goes crashing over and down the hill. They descend like a pack; maybe the school motto has sunk in: 'together everyone achieves more'.

It all starts with the feet. The boys start to kick him. Blows rain in on his legs, body and head. He curls into a ball screaming for them to stop, but nothing will stop them now. Kicks turn to stamps and some jump up and down on his legs; others start to pummel him with their fists, taking turns at striking him. Shane drops on top of him and starts to thump him. The older boy tries to rally and turns his face up to look at Shane, in order to start fighting back, but a boot smashes down into his face and breaks his nose, another kick swings in from the side and lifts his head off the ground as if it was a football. It thuds back on to the ground, but they are not finished yet; they are pulling and ripping off his clothes and it looks as if they intend literally to tear him to pieces.

Whether it was one of the boys who was taking part who turned tail, or someone had followed on behind, we don't know, but word has reached the teachers. They are running out from the main building towards them. The older boy is now covered with blood and mud. He has been pushed into the water, it is shallow not deep, the weeds and rushes at its edge are crushed by the boy's body and his head is now in the water, face down. The bellows of the teachers are now loud, as they have almost reached the lake. Shane is laughing at the boy and the approaching men. The younger boys all separate. Andy Smith is second or third to reach the body of the boy. His colleagues wave him on.

'Get Shane, we'll look after him.'

Two of the teachers are now pulling him out of the water and starting CPR. They can't even tell who it is they are trying to save; blood, mud, torn clothes, a face swollen beyond recognition.

Andy sprints on after Shane as he disappears into the woods.

*

As the others arrive he takes his weight off Shane. Andy is near breaking point. 'You little monster.' He is panting hard for breath. 'Only God's going to change you. We've tried everything for you. There's nothing I can do.'

As the others grab Shane, Andy looks like a man very tempted to take his own retribution out against the boy and barely trusts himself to be in his presence.

'There's nothing we can do with you.' He storms off.

It is the last that Shane sees of him for years, and the last he sees of the school.

Andy Smith tells the later enquiry, 'What is really disturbing about Shane is that he told me over and again he wants to kill, that's the word he uses, "kill". He actually dreams and fantasises of ways to kill police officers in particular; to kill anyone who is an authority figure. He wants to kill, he is bitter and evil to the core.'

Shane is expelled from Elemore Hall, the school where you go if you are expelled from other schools. He is sent to a special secure unit in Aycliffe, the place where the Jamie Bulger killers were later to be sent. It has the highest level of security for children between the ages of ten and 17.

RESPECT

Each year that goes by brings change. At 12 years old on admission to Aycliffe Secure Centre, he is asked to write down his name and address. He can't. At first the security workers think he is being awkward, but he's not; he cannot read or write, or even sign his name. When he says he skipped school, he really meant it, you could count on one hand the number of days he attended in a year. When they ask him his address he doesn't know it, why should he? He knows where it is, and how to get there. He has never needed to tell anyone else where he lives; certainly not the police, they all know it off by heart. He still doesn't learn to read in the Aycliffe centre because he is committed to fighting against the system in its entirety, he will not co-operate on anything.

He is locked up, he is released, he commits bucket loads of offences, goes back to court, and back to being locked up, in a constant cycle. Nothing changes except that he starts to grow. At 16 he cannot be sent back to Aycliffe; it is a secure school, and at that age his formal education has come to an end. Eventually Shane learns to read and write by himself, self-taught because he will not listen to anyone who would have shown him how.

He is bigger now and no longer tolerates being picked on by other kids. He reflects, years later, that he never felt as if he fitted in, and puts it down to his ginger hair. He may have a point, there is increasing data and research that ginger kids are often ostracised and bullied. However, whatever the facts about that, at 16 he undergoes a very real change. He decides no one is going to take any more 'liberties' with him. He starts to fight, not as kids fight, but for real, fights like his Uncle Robert would get into. In fights like these, ears and noses are bitten off and swallowed so they can't get sewn on again. Limbs are broken so they won't heal, eyes gouged, faces disfigured. Dirty fighting, street fighting, fighting most of us will never see and never want to.

He loves the feeling when he wins, the pleasure of people coming and slapping him on the back, the look of fear in the eyes of some, respect from his peers. His first real fight at 16 is marked by people lining up afterwards to shake his hand. The attention he gets from others is a buzz; the fact is that he wants people to know who and what he is.

He knows he isn't the hardest man around but he is what people call 'extra game'. People know that he is prepared to keep fighting even when it should be over, and to get revenge no matter what.

*

Shane now has even more reason to be in trouble with the law. When not locked up he is still involved in burglary, arson, and car crime, but now he is also branching out into drugs and fighting. He carries four or five large kitchen knives in a special belt around his waist whenever he goes out and he likes using them. He is back in court again and again but now all the soft options are off the table.

Once a young person involved in crime gets to 17 then things change yet again and sentencing can now include being sent to a young offender institution, which is essentially a prison for young people. It is designed to be run with a lighter touch from the guards than adult prison, but they are still very violent places.

He is in and out of every youth offender institution in the North of England, first for what they call short sharp shocks, later for longer and longer sentences, often out for just a few weeks then back inside. The one positive consequence of these regimes is that he is being encouraged to reinforce his ability to read and write. He learns fast and, because he is teaching himself to read, he starts to read everything he can.

He finds a book on the history of Peterlee and because it's his home town he reads it, it makes him laugh out loud.

It started with grand ideas. The government set up the Peterlee Development Corporation after the war in 1948, but things didn't take long to go wrong. The first plans were for tower blocks. The architect Lubetkin, who was brought in by the local labour luvvies, actually wanted to build huge concrete tower blocks in the 'brutal modernist' style. They had plans for an opera house and even brought in a modern artist to build public monuments. However the underground mines meant there would be no tower blocks; the warrens of tunnels underground wouldn't allow any large buildings to be built on top. So the head architect went back home to the capital. There he got the contract to build Tower Hamlets and some other notable examples of his trade. Some see them as unliveable nightmare spaces and a hideous mess; others may see them as a beautiful concrete paradise in the heart of London. Take your pick. If you want to know what Peterlee would have looked like, do a Google on Lubetkin's work at the Cranbrook Estate and Sivill House Bethnal Green or his Dorset Estate in Tower Hamlets. All made increased use of pre-cast concrete façade panels, which may explain why the British Cement Association established the Berthold Lubetkin Memorial Lecture, and the annual Lubetkin Prize.

In Peterlee the modern art monument, The Pavilion, is a large house-like structure that spans a mini lake to give a 'vista for the contemplative'. Well, that's what the town visionaries say, it is seen by others as a graffiti-ridden mess where yobs hang out, and is hated by the residents.

Shane gets angry at the idea that the planners cannot see the obvious, they are so far removed from ordinary people that they do stupid things.

He discovered it gets better. The first town planner, Dr Monica Felton, somehow took time off her job to go off to the Korean War to 'support the North against the US and UK'. When she got back, she was fired from her job as Chair of the Development Corporation, expelled from the Labour Party and threatened with prosecution for treason.

Worse was to come, the ineffectual dreamers were replaced by the corrupt. Some of the leading politicians and political insiders of the day were caught up in scandal. T Dan Smith was another Chairman of the Peterlee Development Corporation. He and the architect John Poulson built cheap housing projects they knew to be of low quality and skimmed money from the contracts. They went to prison.

Shane stops and reads the book again. The people who built the town where he lived went to prison. Unbelievable.

Then something else catches his eye. He had often been to the courts and police station in Peterlee and would have passed the foundation stone set into the wall at the front of the buildings many times. A local politician, Andrew Cunningham, the father of the Labour cabinet minister Jack Cunningham, had formally opened the building. His name was on the foundation stone for everyone going in to the building to see, all the criminals dragged into the building, all the police and lawyers who walked in and out. There it was, set in stone; yet a short while after the opening of the police station Cunningham too was in prison with T Dan Smith and Poulson on charges of corruption.

He howls with laughter.

Shane knows what he is, but now he also knows

what others with power and authority are like too. They might talk down to him but they are no better.

Why should he listen to a word that they say?

*

And one of the biggest incidents for Shane was a chance meeting with a man on The Royal Arms estate. He is known as being 'pretty handy', a hard lad and a tough fighter.

Shane is on a motorbike and driving up the street, passing where the man is standing leaning against a lamppost. There is often a strange protocol on these occasions. If he drives past him without saying anything, it could look as if he is frightened, so Shane slows down, expecting a sort of nod of acknowledgement before going on.

The man is standing drinking from a can of beer but when Shane slows to a stop he looks up and drops the can of beer by accident. Shane looks at him as it splashes his boot. To his shock, the man is shaking visibly. Shane stares at him.

There is panic on the man's face.

'Oh sorry, mate, I'm sorry about that.'

The hairs at the back of Shane's neck stand on end and he knows that he has reached a new level of respect; the people on his own housing estate are scared of him, even the hard lads. From this point his mindset starts to change even further.

A friend is walking with him down the street and points to the man over the road coming out of a pub.

'See him over there, he's hard, him. He's crazy, don't mess with him, Shane.'

Suddenly it's a challenge to him.

'What you telling me that for? What, you think I'm scared?'

So he now feels he has to cross the road to get ahead of the man, then turn back and deliberately bump into him and challenge him.

'What you're doing bumping into me, you?'

It's about as formal a challenge as it used to be in the old days, slapping someone in the face with your glove and challenging them to a duel.

He always thinks about these fights as a way of him being able to 'take someone's name off them'. There is a league table in his head; you tick them off the list as you beat them.

So he progresses from being picked on and pushed around, to having his first fight, and then on to constant fighting and getting more attention. He loves people coming up to him and saying 'that was mad that, you're game, you'.

He thinks, 'Yes!'

There are bigger and better fighters around on the streets, but sometimes they see something that gives them pause. One such man was Paul Venis, who was later to become both the European and the World Heavyweight Champion in K1 Mixed Martial Arts.

He lived in Teesside all his life and crossed Shane's path from time to time. He remembers the time well when a fight started up in the middle of the street, the respective friends on the path at either side of the road. The fight is between one of Shane's cousins and Paul's friend. Shane wants to stop anyone joining in and stands in his newly adopted psycho pose, his eyes popping wide and veins sticking out of his temple and throbbing to some internal beat.

'If anyone joins in, I'll stick this in their neck.'

He is holding a massive screwdriver in his hand.

Normally someone threatening Paul would find themselves on the floor. He has one of the most deadly right hands in the business, in all his future professional fights he never loses and never fails to win by knockout, but as he looks at Shane he finds himself stopped in his tracks. When he looks in Shane's eyes he knows there is something wrong deep inside. First of all, he believes that Shane really will stick the long blade into whoever interferes. He then admits to feeling an unexpected and unprecedented wobble of fear; something alien and unknown to him. He knows that it isn't that he wouldn't beat Shane in a fight, but rather what would happen afterwards. He looks at him and knows that there is madness in him and it is only just below the surface. Anything might trigger it, and if someone does that it will be very real trouble.

For the first time in his life he backs off and lets matters take their course.

Paul Venis isn't the only one who finds themselves

intimidated by the new Shane. Maz and her new husband Benny are becoming worried.

Maz is sitting in The Royal Arms with her friend and neighbour Sharon.

'Shaz, we're going to get another house,' Maz explains.

'You're leaving Peterlee?'

'No, just renting around the corner, Shane's staying though.'

Her friend looks uncomfortable. She takes a big sip from the pint of lager in front of her. It's a busy night, the place is full. Benny is sitting with three of his friends playing dominos in the corner of the bar. Maz and Shaz are just past the point of tipsy, before falling into the business of getting seriously blotto.

'What's the crack? What's going on with your lad?'

Maz's eyes fill up.

'I'm starting to get scared of him Shaz, Benny is bloody terrified, none of the family will come around.'

'I know what you mean.' Her friend shudders. 'He scares the living daylights out of me when I hear him shout.'

'Why do you think we are here every night? We can't be in the house with him. When he loses his temper you look at him and you can see that he doesn't even know himself whether he'll hit me or not. We just to go to bed as soon as we are in to avoid him and just let him do what he wants in the house.

I don't think he would hurt me, but it's a possibility I can't get out of my head.'

Shaz leans over and whispers as if Shane would somehow overhear what she is saying from wherever he happens to be.

'I've heard that he stabbed someone last week.'

Maz looks uncomfortable and nods.

'It's all my fault. If he couldn't have what he wanted, he used to just go crazy, call me names and things like that, and start smashing the house up, so I used to give him what he wanted just to stop him. Then other times I think it wasn't down to me, it's him. Do you know what I mean? Fighting with people, threatening to kill people, threatening to shoot people, threatening to stab people.'

She takes a big swig. The tears are flowing in a steady stream down her cheeks.

'What's wrong with him? Is he mental? Coming out with something like that. You know what I mean? You can't believe your kid's saying things like that. It's awful.'

Having his parents move out is great for Shane, it means not worrying about anyone else. He has developed a passion for violent films of any sort; he'll watch the death scenes repeatedly, looping them non-stop.

This is at a time when the Sun, the Mirror and the Daily Mail all scream headlines blaming killers for imitating things in 'video nasties'. The press is full of dreadful warnings about the effects of violent movies and panics about how it corrupts the minds of the young.

The truth is far more complex. Clearly many people watch violent films and don't become violent, that kind of direct correlation doesn't bear scrutiny. But if someone has a propensity towards that kind of particular behaviour, it can be fed, watered, and will grow.

Shane sits in the dark; the only light is coming from the TV set. He drinks can after can of lager. His hand on the remote rewinds and plays his favourite scenes over and over again from his VHS video collection. He is addicted to films where people are getting stabbed to death and where gangsters do drive-by shootings. It's like a drug rush for him that makes him feel special and alive. His hair stands on end and he thinks, 'Yes! I want to be a gangster.'

He is watching *Goodfellas* every day, especially the scene where Robert De Niro and Joe Pesci are stabbing a man in the trunk of a car, and it's swish, swish, swish; the sounds of the knife going in. At the time he thinks it is realistic but that is because he hasn't yet experienced what it sounds like for real.

His friends are now becoming convinced that something is deeply wrong with him. The night before he was at a party of a lad who has a reputation in the nearby town. Shane still can't understand conversations he had there, and goes over them again in his mind.

One lad, who was meant to be tough, had only been talking to him for a couple of minutes, before shaking his head and walking away. As he does he says, 'You're nuts, you.'

Shane tries to figure out what he had said, and catches up with him, swinging him around.

'What do you mean?'

He can't understand it, he knows it's not just what he says, but rather everyone seems to see something in him.

'You are nuts. You are going to get life'd off.' (A life sentence for killing someone.)

'How, explain it to me?'

The man holds up his hands.

'I can't explain it, but there's something wrong with you and you'll get life'd off, I know you will.'

'Yeah, well, tough.'

As Shane sits in the dark mulling over the events he has a flash of understanding, he suddenly understands that something has changed in him in recent weeks.

If he's going to have a fight, there is no fear at all; even if the other person is armed, fear has dropped out of his life and nothing bothers him, not only is there no fear of being hurt, there is no fear at all of any consequence by police or jail sentences.

As he switches off the video and he is left alone in the dark he understands that he has lost something else, there has been a fundamental shift.

For all his previous affection for family and friends, he discovers that he now isn't concerned about anyone at all. He loves no one. If anyone close, even his mam, were to die tonight, he wouldn't even shed one tear. He suddenly understands that he is dead inside and it feels great, it isn't something to worry about; rather it is true liberty. He can do, and will, do exactly what he wants. He creates a mantra in his head, a growing creed that he amends and learns as he thinks it through. He says it over and over in the dark, and it feels somehow to him as if his eyes are glowing bright in the dark room with anticipation. He is sure if he looked in a mirror he would be gleaming, light streaming from his eyes. The creed is simple:

'It doesn't matter how big and tough you are, 'cos I might not be the biggest and hardest man, but I'll win. No matter who you are, I'll win and you better kill me now because if you don't I'll come back and I'll kill you. I will win in the end, 'cos I will hunt you down and I will get you.'

He repeats the mantra over and over again until the first hint of morning arrives, the greyness of a cheerless dawn begins to push out the night, and it leaves no promise for the coming day. He sees it and knows it's going to be bleak and stormy. It makes him smile.

THIRTEEN

2000

REMAND

What happened next is subject to argument over who said what, and did what to whom. This is Shane's account.

Shane, Ronnie and Pete, a large lad who looked older than his 14 years, are out in a car. The car might have been legal or stolen, no one can quite remember. They are searching for Smithy, a lad on the estate. He unwisely and untruthfully has been telling people on the estate that after a fight he chased Ronnie away with a stick. Ronnie is furious and determined to show him face to face whether he is scared of him or not. This is important stuff, reputations are everything, and so they tour the street. At last Ronnie spots him and the car screeches to a stop. Ronnie jumps out.

Smithy panics and looks ready to bolt.

'Hey you, you lying git.'

Ronnie has now squared up to him.

Shane and Pete amble out, lean on the car and decide to watch.

'Ronnie, he's an idiot, he didn't run.'

'He's like a rabbit caught in the headlights, mate.'

Ronnie starts to lay into the man. After a while, he stops, picks him up off the ground, and throws him over a small hedge into a garden. A driver going past has seen what has happened and pulls up. As Ronnie, Shane and Pete are about to go off, a massive mountain of a man gets out of his car. He clearly has decided to play the Good Samaritan; he walks up to the man lying on the garden.

'Are you alright?'

Smithy groans.

Shane walks up to the man before he can interfere any further.

'Uh, yeah, he's alright. Go on, on your way… Go on. Get going.'

The newcomer persists.

'Are you alright?'

'I said, you need to go on mate, it's nothing to do with you.'

Shane's eyes are nearly popping out on stalks as he out-stares the man, who reluctantly backs down. He walks off, muttering to himself.

Shane starts up the car and Ronnie jumps in.

As they are driving away Pete sticks his feet up over the back of the seats in front.

'Watcha think of these, eh? Whoa, look at me new trainers.'

He waggles them.

Shane slows down.

'When did you take them? You nicked Smithy's trainers, you idiot? That's robbery.'

Shane hadn't seen him take them, neither had Ronnie.

'It's straight off robbery; you get like seven to ten years for that. Get them off.'

Pete complains, 'What you doing?'

'I'm giving them back, the other bloke was a witness, I'm not doing time for this.'

He drives round to Smithy's house and goes up to the door. He hammers on it. An older man answers, the lad's grandfather. Shane hands over the trainers.

'Your lad's left these behind after a run in with my mate.'

He glances over his shoulder; Ronnie is in the car watching.

'Tell him not to be so silly next time.'

He goes back to the car.

'Sorted.'

Pete puts on his old manky half rotted trainers.

'It's a shame, I liked them.'

It's later in the day when the police stop him in the street as they drive down the road back on to their estate. A car pulls up in front of them, lights come on in the car behind them, both are unmarked cars, they are swarmed with police officers and dragged off to the station.

It takes a while for the penny to drop. Shane thinks

at first they are up on a robbery charge but it's worse: its kidnapping, robbery and intimidation charges.

Smithy's granddad has complained to the police that Shane came to intimidate them. Smithy, the trainer shoes boy himself, has told the police a rather garbled account of what happened. He said that he had been beaten up for no reason whatsoever, stripped, dumped into the boot of their car, held prisoner, taken out, tortured, put back in the car and finally dumped in the middle of a street.

Ronnie and Shane are held on remand, banged up at the youth offenders at Northallerton for a full eight months while the police investigate. Pete is only 14 so escapes a custodial remand. Eventually the police admit there is no evidence whatsoever. The man had all his clothes and his trainers, so the scene of crime officers could check for fibres, blood and DNA in the boot of the car. However there were no fibres, no bloodstains and no bits of skin, hair or other gubbins that would give any indication that he was ever there. Furthermore the boot hadn't been cleaned but was messy, stained and as horrible as teenagers' cars usually are. Conclusion: trainer boy is definitely lying. The police reluctantly let Ronnie and Shane go.

Shane having been locked up for a full eight months is spitting blood and determined to make someone pay.

It is a nice sunny day and people are outside sunbathing, drinking and having a BBQ. Shane is out on his motorbike; he pulls around the corner and sees that Smithy's family are all out in their garden, about ten of them. Shane's cousin is riding on the back. Shane pulls up to give the sunbathing clan the evil eye. Around his waist is his usual pack of knives, arranged in order, packed tight, and strapped to him.

One of the braver (or foolhardy) members of the group spots Shane and mouths, 'You're a dead man.'

Shane revs the bike and shoots off down the street, leaving the man feeling very brave. At the end of the street Shane swaps places with his cousin, the bike tears back down at speed towards the family in their garden.

The idea is to screech to a stop and for Shane to jump into the garden. It nearly goes to plan but the bike is going faster than Shane expects as he jumps off, and so he ends up at a staggering run. He is forced to leap the fence and the knives stab into him. He grabs the largest knife, which is poking into him, and then charges the ten members of the family. Shane swears he was there to scare the living daylights out of them but now he is in their garden running at them knife in hand, shouting, 'I'm going to kill you all.'

The kids, the grannies and the women all scream and most run into the house. Shane wouldn't have done anything to the kids and grannies but considers the men fair game.

'You're all going to die.'

His eyes bulge as he unwittingly does a hulk impression.

'People are going to die.'

120

All the men run away, leaving a couple of little children in the garden looking up at the big man with the ginger hair and bright red face. Meanwhile men are escaping, jumping over fences from garden to garden. Inside the women's faces are pressed up against the windows staring out.

In the street Shane's cousin is doubled up in laughter. Shane walks back down the garden path and, after carefully locking the gate behind him, he jumps on the bike and they zoom off.

Although it was the end of it for now, this incident wasn't over, it was to be the reason why later Shane finds himself up on one of his charges of attempted murder.

HEAD TO HEAD

Shane is in Hartlepool about five miles up the coast from Peterlee with Taz and Pete; they are selling stolen goods from their burglaries, having a quiet word with some people they think might be interested in buying a dodgy video player.

Suddenly Jon Burns and his friends arrive. Jon, who has only just come out of prison, is a local hard lad and seems keen on his territorial rights. They are interested in the video, but not in paying for it. They grab hold.

'We're having that.'

They push Taz away and hang on to the video.

Shane and the younger boy are across the street.

'Whoa, get your hands off.'

Pete looks at Shane.

'Go on lad, I have your back.'

The young lad brings out a baseball bat that he has hanging inside his coat and runs over to the gang who have just stolen the video. Shane jogs over too.

'Don't think you're taxing us.'

Taxing is a term for stealing drugs, stolen goods

or money from another criminal because you have more 'power' than them; essentially because you are higher up in the pecking order of crime.

Pete is swinging the bat at the gang. The biggest of them, Jon Burns, just smiles and pulls out a short-handled mell hammer, the type used in demolition work. The head is a solid thick chunk of metal.

Shane and the others didn't expect this and suddenly it looks like Pete is out of his depth. Shane pulls out a nine-inch kitchen knife and runs at Burns who swings his hammer at the boy.

It misses Pete, who jumps back, leaving the two big men to face each other off. Shane lunges in but Burns beats him to the punch: the hammer connects with Shane's head with what should have been a killing blow. Shane is stopped in his tracks and for a moment is rocked, everything spinning. Everybody pauses, waiting for Shane to hit the floor. It is a moment frozen in time. Then everything moves at once. Somehow Shane can still move and he brings his knife down into the top of Jon Burns' head. The blade snaps off and Shane is left holding the handle.

When he looks at Burns, he wonders at first if he is seeing things, given that he is dizzy from the blow and is feeling dislocated from what is going on. Burns must have been bending forward slightly at the time because the blade has penetrated the crown of his head and come out from under his eyebrow: it's just there, stuck. Burns rises up, roars in anger and then tries to swing his hammer. Everyone is looking at him, he's like a character from a horror movie, he should be dead, but he's trying to fight. People in the street are screaming and running.

Burns' friends try to get him to sit down. One of them is ashen faced as he looks at Burns. Blood is pouring down, it always does from a head wound. Burns seems to understand what is in his head and the reason the blade is sticking out above his eye. He grabs the top of the broken blade on top of his head and pulls it out, cutting his hands as he does. There is literally a fountain of blood spurting out of his head.

Shane's friends are looking at him and trying to figure out how he is still standing after being hit on the head with a demolition hammer. Sirens can be heard; the police station is only a few hundred yards away.

'Run.'

They sprint away across the road and up a side street.

Jon Burns staggers around waving his hammer and tries to chase them.

Shane and his friends are laughing and shouting as they get away from Burns and the arriving police.

It is a story of two bone heads, one has taken a blow from a mell hammer that should have cracked it open like an eggshell, the other head has a knife sticking out of it, and both are still running around. If it were in a novel or film it would be laughed at but, as they say, life is stranger than fiction.

'Without a doubt, this could have killed him,' says Detective Inspector Steve Bakewell. 'He came within centimetres of death.' Pens scribble away. That sounds like a ready-made headline; the press love it.

The press conference is filled with local reporters but the nationals are catching on to the story too. Some local stringers will pass the story on as soon as the conference is over. Inspector Bakewell continues in a deep measured tone to stress the facts.

'Paramedics treated the injured man at the scene before he was taken to Hartlepool General Hospital by ambulance. Miraculously, the nine-inch bladed knife bounced through his skull, missing his brain.'

He doesn't mention Burns by name, or the fact that he had just got out of jail and was trying to tax Shane's gang, or that he had hit Shane over the head with a hammer. There is only ever one villain in a story and only one hero. The events require that Shane is the outlaw (which of cause he is) and Burns is the innocent poor victim (which of course he isn't). But that is the way it works. Black and white is better than shades of grey. People like to know who to boo, and who to cheer.

Shortly afterwards Shane is arrested and questioned. Although there are eye witnesses, none of the protagonists seem willing to talk about what happened. The police case is not quite strong enough for them to charge him and they are forced to release him while they gather evidence. After all, Shane has only just come out of eight months on remand despite no evidence. This time they must be careful.

BLOOD

A couple of weeks later as the police start to get the evidence together for a re-arrest, Shane is having trouble selling a whole load of ecstasy tablets he has bought. Normally they go well in the clubs, 'gets you a good buzz', as he puts it, 'for the weekends'.

But people aren't buying. Someone has passed the word around the room that the speckled dots in the pills are heroin, and heroin wasn't a big thing in Peterlee at the time, so people are a bit wary.

Since he can't sell them, he goes into The Royal Arms to give the tablets to a pal and to say, 'Have a good night on me.'

As he goes in, he doesn't know that the Smithy family, with whom he had recently had the run-in, are connected to a hard man called Booth. The Smithy story has grown as people tell it over and over. It has now become widely believed that Shane had threatened the 80-year-old granny of the clan and was going to stab her until stopped by the good and brave men of the family.

Booth, the friend of their family is drinking in The Royal Arms, believing the lie that Smithy's family had told him. Shane has been warned that the story has grown and Booth was showing an interest in what happened. Shane decides to put him right.

Shane goes over to where Booth is sitting with his friends. Shane sees that he is wearing a long leather coat like a wannabe bad guy out of Buffy the Vampire Slayer. Before Shane can say anything Booth points the finger.

'I want a word with you.'

The room goes quiet. Conversations stop, people pretend to take a drink from their glasses while surreptitiously watching carefully what happens.

Shane sits down, wary that it might look like he is being ordered about.

'You threatened an old woman with a knife, who do you think you are?'

'I didn't threaten a granny, that's a lie.'

'Think you are tough, do you?'

Booth stares at him, on either side the men with him are sneering and prepping for trouble, all three are giving him the eye.

For Shane the room grows hot, and he knows that everyone is watching and waiting. Some of them are waiting for him to back down, but the others know that he could go full psycho at any second. Leather man Booth has a reputation, he is 'known', his two friends are 'known' too. Their trouble is that they remember the younger Shane, the boy, but that isn't who is sitting in front of them now.

Shane's life at that time is all about reputation, it

means his life. He would die rather than back down.

He looks to the side and thinks, 'If I don't do anything here, all them there are going to go around the estate and tell everyone that I got pulled up by this lad and I didn't do anything about it.'

He makes the choice there and then that he has to make an example of Booth. Just as Shane is making up his mind on what to do, Booth says the worst thing he could.

'You want to mess with the big boys, do you?'

Shane snaps, he puts his face in Booth's face, and shouts out,

'No. No. No. You're messing about with the big boys. Get outside 'cos I'm gonna kill you.'

Shane gets up and goes out the front door and gets his knife ready, pulling out the biggest from around his waist, and waits.

Inside everyone's trying to stop Booth and his friends from following.

Shane stands in the dark bouncing up and down on the balls of his feet, getting pumped up, but no one comes out.

Eventually Shane loses his patience and opens the door of the pub to see what is going on.

In the foyer a man is holding Booth back.

'He means it. Don't go out there. He'll kill you, matey, he'll kill you.'

Booth is pushing forward, the leather coat billows out behind him from a blast of cold air blowing in from outside. Behind him his mates follow at either side, bemused at what is going on. Others from the bar are out trying to stop him. Booth is shouting,

'Move out the way, I want to do him.'

Someone's voice rings out over him:

'Leave him. Leave him. You've warned him. Move out the way.'

So the lads just step aside. A last one tells Booth,

'We've told you, lad, don't go out there.'

The door starts to swing open and Shane has got his nine-inch kitchen blade ready.

Booth comes out of the door, maybe he poses a bit, maybe he is caught flat-footed but he isn't ready for what happens next because immediately Shane stabs him straight through the top of his chest. As fast and as simple as that. It goes in without a sound, the man just looks surprised and looks down at it in disbelief, and then when Shane pulls it out he hears what it is really like to stab someone. There is a squelching, slurping noise, and Booth just drops straight to the floor. It is nothing like the movies, the blood comes out as fast as if someone has opened a tap. The other two men pull out their own knives and drop into fighting stances. Now there are many martial arts that teach you how to fight and how to defend yourself against a knife. The only real answer is don't. Don't ever face someone with a knife because it is a lottery. Knives can be held blade backwards; the sharpened edge along the outside of the arm, great for slicing a fist or a kick coming towards you. They can be held in the traditional way, pointy end forward, the way people practise against it in the dojo, but if the wrist rotates even by a slight amount everything changes, everything you learn goes out the window.

They are at either side of him, one man feints with a short stab and springs back as Shane reacts, and the other is in as soon as Shane moves. Shane rotates to try and shift the dynamic of the group; he can't be exactly in the middle, he must be closer to one. They try the feint and attack again; these lads have been in knife fights together because they know what they are doing but they are repetitive, they try the same thing again too many times. Most likely it was due to nerves, they should know better; when adrenaline shoots around your system and your blood is pumping hard, it changes everything. The dojo can never prepare you for it, you react differently, and training can easily fall away. It is the will of the person that dominates the fight or flight response.

This time Shane anticipates another feint by the first man and moves on the second man as he comes in. He swings his knives at the second attacker, the blade whistles a fraction of an inch away, any closer and it would have gone straight through his temple. A powerful blow, a truly killing blow.

The second man is shocked and the reality dawns on him. His friend Booth is down on the floor in a pool of blood and he was almost down there with him. He moves back, and then further still. The other man sees what has happened and their eyes meet. There is a slight nod.

'Okay mate. We're done.'

Shane says, 'You're going to die. I want you more than him lying down there. Nobody pulls a weapon on me. I'm gonna get you.'

The flight response wins; they run. In the distance the ambulance and police can be heard. One of Shane's friends shouts out,

'Get out, Shane.'

He turns and he runs. Someone has a car ready; he jumps in and is away before the police arrive. The ambulance men get there and do their best. Booth has a drip attached and the wound is being staunched. An officer asks,

'What are his chances?'

They shrug, it's tight, it's touch and go. Another officer is talking to control to get the scene of crimes team there fast and to speak to the gold response team leader, the on duty superintendent who handles major crimes incidents. Things move relatively fast, everything must be done procedurally and in order; warrants approved and signed, armed response teams assembled. For those in the police who know Shane, this is the event they were both expecting and dreading.

It looks like it will be murder, the man in the ambulance is in a very poor condition, he has lost a lot of blood, the chest wound is massive, a nine-inch kitchen blade produces a terrible wound. If the knife had been left in, he would have stood a better chance as it seals the wound to some degree but, pulled out, the man stands very little chance. Internal organs are punctured and leaking inside, blood vessels sliced open. His blood pressure has dropped to virtually nothing; the blood supply to the heart and head is compromised. The ambulance men furiously try to get massive amounts of fluids in and compress the wound to stop the bleed. Even if they are successful at staunching the bleed, the worry is the internal damage they cannot see without a scan or treat without an emergency team in theatre.

The raid on Maz's house is relatively swift. Police land with guns, the street's sealed off, a heavy battering ram knocks the lock and hinges straight off the door and the police pour in.

Maz and Benny lie face down on the floor, hands on their heads while the place is searched in case Shane is there. His own house is receiving the same treatment.

Shane is now thrust into the news, the evidence is back from the Jon Burns incident, the prints have been identified on the knife and there are now warrants for two attempted murders. A huge manhunt begins. The gears are stepped up as all the regional police forces target his capture. Shane is the most wanted man in the region, and he is on the run.

He knows that he is going to face a big stretch in jail and he goes wild.

In his head, he gives up on life. No one can now come in front of him without the risk of getting stabbed or killed.

SIXTEEN

2000

TAX

Shane is still stealing anything that might turn a profit to keep him on the run. He also decides that if he is going to be put away, he might as well settle a few scores along the way. One day he is riding pillion on a motorbike and sees a brand new bike and thinks, 'I'll have that.'

He jumps off, and still has his helmet on as he tries to snap the lock.

He hears a voice from above and looks up.

'What do ya think y'a doing?'

He takes his helmet off to see who is shouting at him. Ever the relatively polite thief, he shouts back.

'I'm nicking your bike.'

All at once Shane recognises him. Who should it be but a man who attacked his mam some years before. Shane had been doing a stretch in jail at the time and wasn't around to defend her. It was one of the things on his list to be settled at some point, but their paths had not crossed. The man's head is poking out of the top window of the three-story block of flats.

Shane starts jabbing the air at the man.

'You. You… You're going to get it, you.'

The man is indignant. 'Who do you think you are?'

Shane has now swapped his fairly pleasant 'Jack the lad' demeanour for his psycho persona.

'You don't remember who I am? You beat my mam up, didn't you?'

He runs to the entrance to the block of flats and starts booting the door in. The man is terrified, suddenly realising who Shane is, and knowing that he is on the run for attempted murder. He literally barricades himself and his family inside, hauling chests of drawers and furniture to block the door while he calls the police.

Sightings of Shane are springing up all around the region; he is all over the place going absolutely and totally crazy.

The days tick by and he finds he has been on the run for a good three or four weeks. In some ways it seems like it is even longer. Though Booth, the man who he stabbed, has pulled through and is off the critical list the police are treating Shane as being a 'severe risk to the public'. They are blocking off areas around the town, often blocking full roads off. Bobby cars are piling into the cordoned areas and raiding houses. There seems no logic at times when people that Shane doesn't even know are raided. He figures that the police are using him as an excuse to raid a lot of houses of other interest to them. You know the sort of thing:

'…We have a warrant to search this property to see if Shane Taylor is hiding here. What? No? He isn't here? Hang on, what are these bags of white powder doing in your sideboard? Alright, chummy, you're nicked.'

It's easy really; get a nark on your patch to ring in with a tip against someone you know is dealing. Get them to say Shane is hiding out there. Next minute it is written up as a highly placed intelligence source and the bobbies are shooting off to the magistrates to get them to sign the warrant.

Shane is in fact hiding out in a flat; it belongs to a friend who isn't declaring it as his because he is subletting from a tenant and then in turn re-subletting to Shane, no rent book, no papers, no records.

Moving around town is best done on a motorbike, the rules are simple: wear a helmet when you leave the house and don't take it off until you are back inside. Importantly make sure that you don't tell anyone where you are going in advance, then you should be safe enough.

Then the police themselves accidentally do something to make it easier for Shane to avoid capture.

One of Shane's friends tells him about it as they are having a drink in a house. They are sprawled across the sofa and chairs watching telly when he says,

'They lifted me today and questioned me about you.'

'Oh, aye?'

'But the thing was while I was in the car I saw your picture.'

Shane sits up.

'In the car?'

'Aye, I reckon they all have them. Thing is it says "armed and dangerous".'

Shane feels a surge of pleasure: 'armed and dangerous'.

'But it also said, "no approach, do not attempt to arrest without back-up".'

The implications sink in immediately.

'So if they spot me, they won't get straight out to arrest me?'

'No, they are not allowed to. Not without armed back-up.'

'And how long will it take for them to do that?'

'Dunno, but I bet you have half an hour.'

Shane lifts another can up and takes a sip. He is grinning as he thinks about how much of a run-around he can give the police.

'As long as I can leg it, I should stay on the lam?'

They drink some more and Shane leans forward.

'Can you let everyone know, anyone arrested for anything, keep their ears open. I want to know whatever they are talking about, everything. Get them all to ring you and pass it on to me.'

And so what the police don't realise is that Shane is getting fed back information. Whenever they are arresting criminals for different crimes – nothing to do with him – those who have been arrested are listening in, hearing things and passing back what is going on. He is getting messages straight back saying,

'Aye, Shane they've still got big pictures of you posted to the dashboards.'

Or, 'This is what they were talking about.'

Or, 'This is what they were saying.'

While he is on the run, he has on occasion seen police cars spot him while he is on the street and just drive off. They drive away pretending that they didn't see him and call in for support. He on the other hand waits until they've gone and, playing the same game, pretends that he didn't see them either, so they don't think he's clicked on. He saunters off 'til out of sight then runs – does one – and then he's out of the area by the time the response teams arrive.

One of the problems Shane is facing is that he can't sign on to get his benefit, obviously, or the police would come, so he is running out of money. His only route to money is crime. However the risks now of doing burglaries are too great, so it becomes an easy decision to turn to taxing.

When you tax from criminals, take their drugs or take their cash, they can't exactly report you to the police.

So off he goes and taxes a few people. One of them is his good friend Pete. Shane is determined, he needs money, he regrets what he is about to do, but he goes into the house in Horden. As he lets himself in, there are around seven lads lying around on a bed, and a few on chairs, getting stoned.

'Hey, Shane, how'ya doing, man.'

They are all as high as kites.

Shane sits on the floor. On the sideboard, there is a huge roll of money with several elastic bands stretched around them.

'You lads chillin', okay?'

'Hey, you wanna smoke?'

'Nah, I'm fine.'

Shane nods over to the sideboard.

'A lot of money on there.'

Pete looks pleased, he is proud of his success.

'Yeah, man.'

Shane gets up.

'Give us a look.'

Pete takes in an enormous drag from the joint.

'Oh yeah, I've loads there.'

Shane allows the knife he is carrying up his sleeve to drop down into his right hand, which is hidden next to the sideboard. He grabs the roll of cash, thousands of pounds, with his left.

'Cheers.'

He puts it in his pocket and says, 'You're taxed.'

Pete laughs.

'Shut up man. What you doing?'

He tries to rise from the mattress but Shane pushes him straight back down and brings the knife out.

Shane is looking really strangely at them, and they realise that it's all really happening, it's serious. He looks at all the lads and they just sit there. He waves his knife at each of them in turn.

'Any of yous tell the police on me or tell anyone about this I'm going to kill you. Do you understand? '

There are various shout outs:

'It's nothing to do with me, Shane.'

'It's now't to do with me either.'

They are utterly terrified.

Pete is shocked that his friend would tax him. Shane has the good grace to feel guilty as he jumps on his bike and heads off into the night.

RUN

Desperate to settle old scores while he still can, the attacks mount up over the subsequent days, and the police are chasing every lead. However his network of informers still keeps him briefed. He gets phone calls saying that police are blocking off whole sections of Peterlee and raiding houses looking for him. He had been on the run before, but never like this. He is spotted by a patrol car. He knows that he is on a 'don't approach' but the response is lightning swift and he barely gets away, hiding in an alley as they stream into the street, car after car. It is getting very, very close and feels like it's only a matter of time.

He loses the flat because of the upset over his taxing activities. Those friends who remain close are under constant surveillance by the police. His family are out of bounds too, so he is forced to sleep in a car. Two of his friends are with him. One of them is meant to be on sentry duty as the others get some sleep for their watch.

It actually isn't that his friends let him down but something simple he hadn't taken into account. The windows steamed up. It is April, there are cold nights and the breathing in the car mists the cold glass.

The officer who spots them is on a routine drive

around the streets of Peterlee.

'There is someone in there.'

He calls the index plate of the car in, it is owned by someone tagged as a friend of Shane. The control desk alerts the gold command and the chief inspector on duty alerts the armed response and wakes the gold superintendent at his house. It is the middle of the night. Their task is difficult, it might be Shane, but it might not. If the officers go in and it is Shane and someone is injured there will be hell to pay, if on the other hand Shane isn't there, then the budget will fly out of the window for nothing. In the end it is a no brainer; public safety comes first.

The street is sealed off. The armed response team are in place. The decision must now be made about clearing the nearby houses in case a rogue bullet hits a sleeping householder. But to empty the houses will no doubt alert the occupants in the car. The man on sentry duty must have been dozing off because no alarm is raised inside the car. The decision is made to keep the armed response team back at the end of the street. All the officers there are wearing stab vests and helmets, expanding batons are drawn. Every door to the car is covered.

A flashlight shines into the car, full in the face of Shane as he sits in the driving seat. The radio sparks to life. 'It's him, confirm, Shane Taylor is in the car.'

Fists hammer on the windows.

'We have you surrounded, come out with your hands up.'

For a moment the sleepy Shane is amused, it sounds like an American Western. Then the reality of it hits him. His head still hurts from the hammer attack, although two months have passed since it happened. He pulls himself together and starts the car up. He realises that he is wedged in so if he is to get out he will need to ram the car in front, then reverse at force into the car behind to see if he creates enough space to get the car out.

The windows are being thumped and everyone is shouting. It somehow doesn't seem worth it. The police are screaming for him to come out, his friends are screaming in shock as they wake from whatever dreams they were in, to living in a real nightmare.

All at once Shane stops and switches off the engine.

He thinks, 'You know? Sack it!'

There comes a point when there is nowhere to run, no more options and no plan.

So he opens the door and gives himself up.

Hands grab the keys to the car, doors are opened, everyone dragged out, and Shane hears a voice put him under formal arrest.

'Shane Taylor, I arrest you on the charge of attempted murder, you do not have to…'

The voice fades away as Shane is slammed face down on to the ground and his hands grabbed behind him and slapped into handcuffs. The gravel of the road digs into his face. Lights are coming on in the streets as households are woken. Someone kicks him hard, then another. The report will later explain that he resisted an attempt to take him into custody.

He had been arrested on two separate charges of attempted murder. Shane stabbed both men with nine-inch knives. One through the chest, aimed straight at his heart but deflected by bone. The other was stabbed in the top of his head with the blade sticking out four inches below, through his eyebrow. These were not defensive blows, Shane aimed to kill. However the charges were knocked down from murder to Section 18, going with specific intent to cause harm and threatening to kill.

In reality charges of attempted murder never get convictions; all the person has to do is to say that they never intended the person to die. How can you prove beyond a reasonable doubt that a person intends to kill rather than injure? So Section 18 is the normal plea bargain, the reduced charge, if the victim doesn't die. How Burns and Booth didn't die is a miracle, a fraction of an inch, the slightest of difference in movement, and both would be a different story.

He is sentenced to a mere four years nine months in prison. He thanks his solicitor and barrister for all their work, he expected far worse.

Given he is approaching 20 at this point he must start his sentence back in a youth offenders institution until he is old enough to go to adult prison.

NORTHALLERTON

Shane decides from day one that he will not conform. If someone says sit, he stands, if they say it is day, he'll say night. He is also determined to immediately challenge any other inmate who gets in his way. Yet for all his time in and out of homes and other youth offenders institutions he can still be naive.

There has been a fight, a routine type of fight, not over a big grudge, not over an issue. It is over fast but Shane does something he has never done before or since, which is he turns his back as he turns to leave the cell. There is a sudden shock of pain; the other prisoner has hit him with something over the back of his head. Shane staggers sideways into the bunk beds and only just keeps his balance. The prisoner throws another punch but Shane recovers enough to jump back and push the fist away. Every time a fist is thrown, he reacts on autopilot and pushes it away again. The dizziness, at first overwhelming, is fading. A fist swings towards him and, crack, Shane has ducked under it and hammered his fist into the prisoner's face, tearing open the skin under his eye and bridge of the nose. Snot and blood spurt out everywhere and he falls flat on his back, out completely cold.

Someone whistles; the prison officers are arriving. Shane steps out of the cell and others crowd around him engaging in casual chat as if it was nothing to do with them. They ignore the officers and look shocked when they see what has happened in the cell. The guards assist the prisoner to his feet as he pulls round. The lad with whom he is padded up in the same cell checks out how he is, then whispers,

'Listen, sunshine! This isn't the end. Know what I mean. It's not the end, Shane will have you.'

The prisoner goes pale, the reality of fighting with Shane is just dawning on him and he has started to feel very worried, as indeed he should.

A few days later Shane is talking to Ronnie Coles from Peterlee who is banged up on the same wing. Ronnie is a close friend of Shane's; they have shared hundreds of burglaries and fights together.

Shane leans over and says,

'I'm going in his cell in a minute. I'm going to shut the door. Any prison officers, or any inmates try and get in, fight them, whatever, just buy me time.'

Ronnie grins, he likes a scrap. That, by the way, is an understatement – just so we are clear.

'Alright then. No problem.'

They stroll along the walkway. It is free association time. Prisoners are allowed out of the cell, there are pool tables and other activities. Some chill in their cells, some get out and about. The lad who had chosen to pick a fight with Shane was thinking it was safer to keep his head down and out of his face.

The walkways are open on three floors with nets suspended between the floors to catch the jumpers, and also to stop anyone throwing things down on the guards. The stairways at the ends of the floors can be blocked quite easily and the gates at the end of the wings can be obstructed with bodies. People might seem to be randomly talking in groups, but in the next moment could be stopping the guards getting access.

Shane goes in and shuts the door behind him. His friend stands guard outside.

The man is asleep. Shane taps him, a solid finger into his brow.

'Get up. You'd better get up now.'

His eyes spring open and panic fills his face.

He is stuttering. 'I'm not getting up.'

'Well, I'm going to hit you whether you stay there or not, I'm not a coward like you, it's your choice I'll count to ten.'

On five he jumps out of bed and Shane smashes and smears him all over the cell.

The next day the prisoner makes another massive mistake. It is a strange part of human psychology that makes us believe that we can bond through joint adversity, and maybe for some it may work, but not here.

He walks up to Shane and his friends in the exercise yard, he has butterfly stitches across here, and butterfly stitches across there. His face is a patchwork of cuts and bruises. He acts as if he's earned a bit of respect by not naming Shane to the guards.

'Alright lads. I...'

Shane cuts in abruptly.

'What you doing? What you..? Get out you. Go on. Get stood over there on your own.'

Shane is pushing him back away from the group.

'So what? Did you think you were going to get respect for what you did?'

The man walks away, with that embarrassed look that you get when everyone is staring at you and no one is on your side. It's quiet, absolutely silent. Worse still, there is nowhere to walk to. The exercise yard is locked, the guards stand watching and there isn't anywhere to go. Everyone else is in a group; everybody seems to fill the spaces. In the end he stands in the middle by himself, until exercise is over.

For Shane this lesson in the youth offenders prison was one for the future, one better learned here, because in the prisons where he was going you can never turn your back, because if you do someone will bury a shiv in it.

PARANOID

Shane finds youth prison a place to demonstrate his willingness to challenge everything. Believe it or not he even has a fight with a prison officer over a banana. When you go to the serving hatch for dessert you get cake and custard, or you can have fruit. Shane chooses cake and custard, but his friend Ronnie has managed to pick up an extra banana and passes it on to Shane.

A guard spots it.

'Put the banana back.'

'I don't think so.'

'Don't be silly, put it back.'

Shane pulls back the drawstring to his pants and sticks the banana down it, then lets the elastic slap back. Shane challenges the guard.

'What you going to do about it?'

He comes around the table and eyeballs Shane. Neither know what to do next but they end up fighting.

It was one of those stand offs that should be in a movie. It has comedy at its heart because the guard doesn't really want to win and put his hand down

Shane's pants, Shane doesn't want to beat a guard, well, because that has consequences attached. Others enter the fray, and soon Shane is carried out by three guards, kicking and screaming. No one can remember what happened to the banana.

Shane has a saying, every time he loses his temper, 'Sack it' or 'go off it', translation: throw caution to the wind.

Shane goes wild in the youth offenders prison, he runs into people's cells and beats them up, he is fighting all the time. He is a madman. Then an incident outside the area hits the prison hard. A riot had kicked off in a London prison with extensive damage. The London lads are shipped up into Northallerton Youth Offenders Institution from the capital, and a turf war starts. They are meant to be tough; after all, everything is better and bigger in London, the hardest gangs, the biggest criminals; so they must try to establish their dominance in the prison. One lad in particular takes it upon himself to stake his claim. Behind it all, he most likely wants to be shipped out to another prison closer to home, but he is convincingly tough. He runs at people in the yard until he is in their face and spits and curses challenges to them. This is a yard with around 150 convicts. He runs and screams 'Rrrrr.'

People are jumping out of the way and running. Shane is dumbstruck: 'How on earth could people let him get away with that?'

Exercise yards are actually like the gathering of clans. Lads from Middlesbrough, from Peterlee, all the villages and towns each have their own groups; even if they mingle together at times, it's tribal at its heart. Shane is standing with the inmates from Peterlee. He looks at Michael English, Dean's brother, his best friend from Peterlee, and winks. The next moment they shout,

'Right! Come on!'

They run at the Londoner and swing a few punches. All the lads from London jump up at the back of the yard. The rest of the prison stands behind Shane shouting,

'Come on. We've got your back.'

Then the prison officers arrive and break things up, they hadn't interfered before but now they grab Shane and haul him off to the seg. The segregation unit is essentially a limited solitary confinement. Limited in that there are people in adjacent cells who communicate through the pipes. They also have joint exercise times in their own yard. Then, of course, the guards interact with them as well. However it does mean being locked up for 23 hours a day and occupants have to fall back on their own mental strength and resilience. Shane might well have been tough physically but he has been exhibiting poor mental health for some time.

He is constantly in trouble and continually in and out the seg.

When Shane gets out of solitary confinement he believes that he has been treated unfairly. He makes the point later by blaming the Londoner, and decides to see how much effort it takes to stick a metal tray into the side of his head.

Another battle with other transferees is now ongoing, this time with inmates from Bradford. All the new lads have just come in because there was a riot in Bradford, or south Leeds, and they had all been shipped out.

Some of them are piling in to a local lad and the others feel they have to show they are out of order. Shane runs up with a pool cue and goes after one of the Bradford lads. The Bradford boy puts his arm up to defend himself and the cue smashes him straight across the back of his hand, he screams and drops crying to the ground. Shane jumps back into a doorway and acts as if nothing had happened. Everyone else is carrying on the fight. The prison officers run straight past all those who are still fighting, however, grab just Shane, and take him away to the segregation. It makes Shane realise that he is being singled out; his self-righteousness is offended, as he understands that they are all out to get him.

His state of mind is deteriorating further and further. Every cellmate is seen as a threat and usually ends up being beaten to a pulp after a fit of rage. The governor is now becoming really concerned and is desperately trying to find someone who he can put in the same pad (cell). The prison is overcrowded and he needs all the space he can find; it has to be two inmates in that cell.

The answer lies in the newly sentenced inmates that are due to arrive, including Dean. It must have been like an episode from Friends. Shane, Ronnie, Dean and his brother Michael, plus quite a few others too. They might as well have re-named the wing 'The Royal Arms'.

Dean has been given a long stretch for a very serious offence and, since he is under 21, he finds himself in Northallerton as Shane's new padmate. Given the nature of their relationship it was presumed that all would be OK, but it nearly wasn't.

One night Shane is watching Dean as he passes him his food. This is the evening meal before bed and is delivered to the cell. Shane is watching carefully. The night before his food had tasted gritty and he spent the night with stomach pains.

Shane is now six foot six tall, he is solid muscle and beefed up, he works out every day. Dean on the other hand is slight due to a bad diet and various substance habits. He is small, especially compared to Shane.

Suddenly Shane says, 'What's that you've put in my food?'

Dean is now very worried about Shane. He looks and sees that there is a weirdness to him.

'Why would I poison your food? Y'a mad, you.'

'This tastes like it has glass in it.'

'Tell you what mate, gimme your food. If it has glass in it, I'll eat it.'

Shane sits as solid as a statue, his eyes bright with an inner fever, staring at Dean while he eats.

They sit up all night as Dean explains again and

again that they are friends who trust each other before the situation calms down.

December comes around, another highly significant birthday looms. The guards know it, the governor is chewing his nails waiting, and the day finally dawns.

At first light, Shane is off to court for the formalities. He is now 21, the rubber stamp hits the paper and his approval goes through for his transfer to Holme House Prison, adult prison, cons prison. He doesn't go back to Northallerton and everyone starts breathing again, they have been saved from the disaster that is looming on the horizon. Holme House doesn't yet know how dangerous he is.

HOLME HOUSE

In 2001, the Home Office was responsible for Her Majesty's Prison Service. To protect the public, officers, and inmates, it constantly reviewed the level of danger posed by each prisoner. At that time the male prison population was around 70,000, and each of them was placed in a category that reflected their degree of risk. The highest was Double Category A: this was for an exceptional few, such as high-level terrorists or crime boss godfathers. Then Cat A, highest risk inmates, Cat B, those who didn't require maximum security but for whom escape still needed to be made very difficult. Cat C, for those who could not be trusted in open conditions but who were unlikely to try to escape. Finally Cat D for prisoners who could be reasonably trusted not to try to escape and were given the privilege of an open prison. They could be given approval for ROTL (Release On Temporary Licence) to work in the community or to go on 'home leave' once they had served a quarter of their sentence.

At that time there were around 7,000 Cat A inmates placed in one of the nine specialist maximum security prisons. Being a high-risk prisoner doesn't mean that you will be a problem for the system, some of the highest rated Double Cat 'A's will behave themselves most of their time in jail.

Holme House was a purpose built prison, opened in May 1992, and later expanded to include further house-blocks and workshops in the late 1990s. It catered for Category C prisoners – 'those who cannot be trusted in open conditions but who are unlikely to try to escape'.

Typically, but not always, it housed those convicted of minor offences who were serving shorter sentences of no more than a few years in length. Also Category B prisoners coming to the end of their sentence were sometimes downgraded to Category C to prepare them for release.

Shane was in this initial category because he was young and it was thought a Cat B prison might spoil his chances of rehabilitation. The Prison Service is often portrayed as a tough, punishment-based regime but that is far from the truth; yes, prison guards can act tough and respond to violence, but there is a central ethos, at least with governors and senior staff, to rehabilitate and to let men serve their time in a safe environment.

Holme House has a workshop complex and an education department. They have work and training across a large range of skill-based trades: laundry, woodwork, furniture assembly, textiles, large print production, industrial cleaning, painting and decorating, electrical testing and picture framing. The inmates earn, and learn; if they stick in, they can get NVQ qualifications.

The accommodation at Holme House is set in seven self-contained living units called house-blocks, of single and double cells, all with integral sanitation.

Each house-block is in the form of a cross, three wings are cell accommodation and the other arm of the cross is for dining and other functions. The centres of the cross are where the guards control and monitor what goes on. In free association the doors to each arm of the cross are open but, at the earliest sign of trouble, the guards swarm and lock off the gates.

Shane hates it. There is a significant change in the way this adult prison works to what he is used to. While most inmates are serving relatively short sentences, not all of them are, and the fact is that there are old cons, tough old cons, and the whole atmosphere is different to youth offenders. That said, not many in the place are serving time for what was effectively attempted murder as he is, not many have been in so many fights in such a short time or spent so much time in solitary confinement. He comes with a name, others are aware of him. But this is a tougher regime. He tries to find his feet. However, unbeknownst to the authorities, his mental health crisis lies dormant, just submerged beneath the surface. He is in a single cell, but isn't happy, he feels he needs to make a statement, something that will get him moved on to a different prison.

He doesn't realise that if his plan succeeds it will be a move for the worse; that fact escapes him.

He takes his toothbrush and his cigarette lighter

and goes into the slight recess in the cell that is the toilet area. It is out of sight of the hatch in the door, well, barely out of sight. It is night-time and darkness has fallen.

He grabs his shaving razor and pulls out the blade. He sets it on the edge of the sink. The handle of the toothbrush has already been rubbed repeatedly against the breeze-block wall until it has formed to a point.

It only takes one pound of pressure to puncture human skin, so in order to do real damage in stabbing someone with a toothbrush as a makeshift knife, or shiv, you must deliver maximum force with the smallest possible area. It doesn't need to be sharp but it must be pointy. Such a stab once piercing the skin can do enormous damage as it goes deep into internal organs. In many ways it can be more deadly than a knife. A sharp cut can be treated with easy stitches, ruptured breaks in the organs from a shiv are very hard to fix in surgery.

However there are times when you don't want to kill, merely to create terror and scar someone for life, as a sign to others as to how dangerous you are. So a better weapon for that is a makeshift blade.

The lighter melts the back of the plastic toothbrush, the razors go in three at a time in parallel; if you are cut with one of these, it results in three parallel incisions in the skin, the middle pieces of flesh or skin are harder to stitch and more ugly when they heal. They are usually a marker of prison violence. Having such a weapon at your throat is a very real threat because it can cut the artery in the neck in three places, effectively making it impossible to sew and if used in this way it can be lethal and kill very quickly.

Shane finishes the shiv/blade and hides it inside his mattress. The cells get searched if there is a tip off, but there is no padmate to betray him to the authorities and he has never used a weapon before in prison. He thinks it highly unlikely that they will search his cell and find it, now he just has to decide who he is going to take down and use as a hostage.

HOSTAGE

It is B-Wing, on House-Block One; the lad on the walkway outside Shane's cell isn't doing anything in particular. You linger a lot in a prison, unless you can get the chance to take a turn on the pool table or you are heading to the gym to work on your body beautiful. Of course, it is also the time to sort out what drugs you want for the day, avoid people who look at you funny and, especially, avoid anyone you owe money to. Sometimes lingering is as good as it gets. Shane hears a noise from inside the pad and turns; he puts his finger to his lips and goes, 'Shush.'

The huge ginger-headed man looks as if he has a big secret and he is smiling. He tips back his head, as if to say, 'Come here'. The lad has never had any run-ins with Shane but he knows his reputation. It is one of those situations. He looks friendly enough, and he wants to talk to him, but should he go into the cell? If he doesn't, will Shane become angry? He remembers the old TV series with The Hulk, the first one that is, with Bill Bixby, not the cartoons and silly stuff later. David Banner would look stressed and his eyes would gleam as he was on the verge of changing into the creature,

'Don't make me angry,' he would say, 'you wouldn't

like me when I'm angry.' Shane is a bit like that. He has seen Shane go from calm to raging monster in a split second. It was probably good advice, 'Don't make him angry'. The poor fool placidly walks into the cell.

'You a'rite, Shane?'

The door is kicked shut and he is grabbed by the scruff of the neck; in a split second he is face down on the table and his hands are being tied behind his back with a torn bedsheet.

'Shane, what you're doing, man?'

The young lad wonders if it's too early to have his life flash before his eyes: 'Why did he walk in, why did he hang about near a nutter's cell?'

'If you keep still and don't panic, you'll be fine.'

Shane swings him around and he sees the shiv with the razor blades in front of him. He thinks for a second that he is going to wet himself but desperately holds it back. 'If I survive it won't make matters much better if I'm known to all the other prisoners as the man who wet himself.' He groans at what he has just said to himself,'…if I survive.'

'Okay, off we go.' Shane pulls him up.

Shane is standing behind the lad with his arm around his throat. Shane is tall enough to strangle him with ease and squeezes him just enough for him to see spots before his eyes.

The knife is lying on the side of his neck. Shane grips him so hard his artery is pulsing and sticking up on the side of his neck, it might as well have a label on it saying, 'Cut Here'.

Shane opens the door and stands there. He gives a low whistle and an inmate walking on the walkway across the atrium looks over. His mouth falls open as he sees what Shane is doing.

Shane shouts, 'Go on, tell the guards, go on.'

The man runs off. He must have told others too because the news spreads as fast as wildfire. It is uncanny just how quickly things can spread in prison, it's almost like mass telepathy, faces appear at the sides of his door and inmates assemble over on the other walkway directly opposite so they can get a good view.

'Gan on, Shane, cut his throat.'

'What's he done?'

The banter flows, laughter fills the place.

Shane just grins and closes his door. He pulls the hostage back and waits.

Not every rumour that is spread is true, so while the guards hear of it pretty quickly and respond, they don't expect it to be real. Inmates play stunts and jokes. Real violence often disappears as soon as a screw appears. So the guard makes his way to the cell swiftly but not in a panic. He gets to Shane's door and pushes at it. Of course it isn't locked, only guards have a key; once opened they then turn the latch so it can't be fully closed. But something is blocking the door and pushing it back. He opens the observation panel to look inside.

The terrified hostage's purple face fills the frame

and he is on the verge of tears, the knife at his throat is very real.

'I'll f...king kill him, you know.'

The guard slams the hatch shut and calls it in.

The alarm goes off, prisoners must now go back to their cells. Priority One, it's a lock-down, an incident must not escalate so as to involve other prisoners. All the prisoners get back to their own wing from the communal area. The gates from each wing are then packed with officers as the inmates go into their cells. Any officer across the whole site who is free immediately comes to this house-block.

The other house-blocks are all isolated; anyone in the education or work centres must stay there. Any prisoner on a movement, going from one building to another along the roofed and fenced-in cage-like corridors that interlink all the site, must get to their destination fast.

The governor's office is alerted, it is a hostage situation. The officers who are trained negotiators are being brought to the block, the first aid response team has been summoned and starts to assemble. The problem is serious. The cell is impenetrable except by the door, obviously. But what is designed to keep someone in is also great for keeping people out. It is the only way in. If Shane is blocking it with his body and has a knife at the throat of his victim, any forced entry is likely to prove fatal.

Someone in the governor's office is reviewing Shane's file. They are checking on the crimes from before his arrest and his conduct since. They are forming a profile; is the offender likely to kill? Well yes, obviously. Is he able to be talked down? Everything in the file shouts out about his refusal to take instructions, and his hatred of authority figures.

The situation is bad, very bad.

The guard looking in is trying to keep calm, 'trying' being the operative word.

'Are you the negotiator?' Shane asks.

'No.'

'Then go away and get one, I have a list of demands.'

The guard disappears. This is more hopeful, a list of demands. It might be something dumb like a helicopter to land on the roof to transport him to never-never land, or it might be something they can work with.

They don't know, but Shane's list of demands at the moment has only one item on it: pizza, not the rubbish they do in the kitchen, a proper 12-inch stone-baked jobbie, with all the toppings, from a proper take out, hopefully with a bit of doner kebab meat on the top. In hindsight it may be possible to argue that he really hadn't thought it through.

Further down the same house-block, Prison Officer Smith is finishing off association on House-Block One when the alarm goes off. He is on A-Wing at the time. He finishes off putting his prisoners behind the doors and comes back to sign for his numbers when he hears who the hostage taker is. Smith has just started work at the prison but he isn't surprised because he knows all about Shane from the past

He isn't meant to be involved but he makes his way to the cell. He looks through the observation panel and sees Shane and his terrified hostage.

He knows he might get in trouble, but then he might be able to help. He swallows hard and sticks his head in the hatch.

'Hiya Shane. It's Andy.'

Shane looks up blankly. He grips his hostage tighter and sticks the knife into his throat almost to the point of breaking through the skin.

'Andy. Who's Andy?'

'It's Andy Smith, do you remember me from Elemore Hall School days?'

Shane looks again and does a double take.

'Oh! How you doing, Mr Smith? What are you doing here?'

'Oh, I've been doing fine. I'm a prison officer now.'

'Oh great.'

Suddenly the atmosphere totally changes. It's like a chat between old work mates bumping into each other in the street. Andy is purposely ignoring the hostage who now looks utterly bewildered. The officer is desperately trying to establish some sort of common ground and to build a rapport with Shane, and it's working.

It is a real but surreal conversation that goes on for about five minutes before they run out of things to talk about. They have finished all the possible small talk: 'Remember the time at Elemore Hall when you did this? Do you remember the time when you did that?'

'How many years is it now, Mr Smith?'

'Phew, I dunno, about nine years.'

'Nine years eh.'

Andy rolls back around to the young man in question, and says, 'Shane, are you going to let this young lad go?'

Shane looks at him.

'Aye, okay then, as long as it's only you who comes into the cell, Mr Smith.'

They both know what is likely to happen when he lets the lad go. The guards will come in; he'll be in handcuffs, have a few accidental 'falling downstairs' injuries and then be banged up in segregation.

Andy reads his mind.

'I promise you; it'll just be me.'

Andy goes on, 'So put the knife down and stop being silly.'

Shane looks at the knife and his hostage, it's almost as if he has forgotten what he was doing. He gives a big sigh.

'Just wanted a pizza really.'

'I'll make sure you walk down the seg, you know. I promise you.'

Shane sits down, leaving the hostage nervously standing next to him; he doesn't know if it is safe to make a break for it.

'Right. Let him go.'

So he does.

'Gan on then, marra. Get out.'

The lad goes out, totally freaked. Arms grab him and he is whisked away out of sight, presumably to the medical room to be checked over.

Andy comes in.

'I promised you...you won't get mufti'd up (meaning restrained).'

They walk out of the cell together. Inmates are banging on their doors and shouting, they don't know what is happening and are trying to look out of the cracks around the hatches in their doors to catch a glimpse of what is going on.

The other guards let them through and Shane and Andy saunter down to the seg still chatting like mates about the old days, including the time when Shane nearly killed the boy down by the lake.

They walk into the segregation unit and Shane steps into the cell. There is a pause for a few moments.

'A'rite then, Mr Smith, nice to see you again.'

'You too. Shane. You too.'

The door bangs shut.

For a moment Andy stands staring at the door, feeling that Shane is doing the same on the other side, then he walks off. He doesn't know if he is going to be given a medal for ending the hostage crisis, or given a formal warning for breaching standing orders and protocols. Funny old life.

SEGREGATION

Robert Foley is 21 and serving time for grievous bodily harm. Rob isn't really very well in the head, the authorities have a hint of it and it's why he is in solitary, but the depths of his illness lie undiscovered for the time being. In that regard he is very similar to Shane. Rob is bored and is killing time talking into the pipes and then someone speaks back. In a short time they discover they are the same age and both come from Peterlee. They hadn't met before in prison because they were both in different house-blocks.

The pipes run through the whole side of the wing and, as they talk, what Rob thinks of as 'the echoes' travel like ghosts trying to find someone to speak to on the other side. In the segregation unit you don't actually get to see the other prisoners, so you have to talk through the pipes. They call it the 'bogphone'. Essentially all the toilets in the row are in one system. So to speak to someone in another cell you need to first empty the water in the bowl of the toilet. Rob's favourite method is to take the toilet brush and ram it down over and over again. It pushes the water over the top of the U-bend and carries it way. Toilet paper soaks up any remaining liquid. Rob then takes out the soggy mass and puts it in a heap on the floor to flush later. He can't bring himself as some do to use his cup to empty the toilet water into the hand basin. He worries about germs; you have to have some standards after all.

When empty, Rob sticks his head down into the toilet bowl and talks. All the old hands will be doing the same. You need to talk to someone to keep sane.

They are locked up for 23 hours and 20 minutes a day. They are taken to a small yard for 40 minutes, and then moved back so that another solitary prisoner can walk around and get 40 minutes of sunshine. You can't really run because it's so small you would just hit the fence.

Rob has heard of Shane: the name rings a bell to start with and then when he says he used to hang around The Royal Arms it falls into place. Do you know this person from Peterlee? Do you know that person? It's two different circles but they overlap. Rob used to hang around with Hartlepool people and some from Horden. The heads are down the toilets, talking through the pipes about people they might know, chitchat to pass the time.

The months pass, it passes slowly. No one who hasn't tried it can truly understand what it is like being alone 23 hours and 20 minutes a day. You tell yourself that you will not be broken, then reality sets in. There is no television, you are meant to get access to a book a week, meant to get one shower a week too. Meant to… but that doesn't mean it will happen.

Any misbehaviour results in loss of privilege. No showers, no books, no exercise. Twenty-four hours a day completely cut off, with your head down the toilet for your only company.

There are things you can do if you want, if you are dedicated and very patient.

One, get some string.

You have to make your own though; get your blanket, the only one you have, then pick the seams out. It's slow work but you have two things on your side: time and no distractions. Once you have the long piece of cotton you need to turn it into string. If you run short, then take the seams out of your shirt. Harder but stronger, dismantle the seams on the mattress. So what do you do with string? Well the bogphone can be used in a novel way. Get your string, keep tight hold of one end and flush, now this must be timed right. The man in the next cell or further down the block is doing the same. The hope is that the strings get tangled, then with care you pull the string up. You just hope someone else isn't having a crap at the same time in another cell further up the line, then you get lumps of turds in your string.

So why link cells? Well you can pass drugs from one cell to another. Of course then you come to the complexities of who has had what, from whom, and how they are going to pay.

'Hey, you owe me for some gear I gave you in the seg.'

'What gear? Someone else must have pulled it up, it wasn't me.'

All then goes back to the usual methods of

collection, fists or shivs, you are caught and then go back on the seg. Then it all starts again; all the fun of the fair. Not perhaps what the system expects or planned for, but these inmates can put the Colditz lot to shame in their ingenuity.

Drugs can be passed from cell to cell in other ways. Wait till night-time when all the guards are all tucked up off the wing just watching the cameras, then knock on the wall to the next cell. Both of you will then tie a line around a piece of plastic cutlery, usually a knife because it slides under the door easily. You put it under at an angle pointing towards the next cell but leave the back end in towards you until you are ready to kick it. Now hold tight to the loose end and kick it as hard as you can. Both knives fly out from under the doors towards each other and the lines get tangled together as they overlap. It is then an easy job to pull a line from one cell to another and you can tie off a packet of drugs down the line.

If it misses, haul it back and try again. It's a sort of game of shove halfpenny for adults; hours of fun for all concerned.

*

Shane is suffering. First of all he is constantly caught up in daydreams about violence. He plays over and again in his head scenes from the films he used to watch. One day when Smith brings his food into the cell he becomes very concerned. Shane stands looking puzzled and staring at the floor.

'Why are all those white spiders coming in here?'

Shane sees them clearly, large white semi-transparent spiders as if they have never seen daylight. They are all over the floor. He isn't scared, but there are so many of them.

'What spiders, Shane?'

'Them,' he points to the floor, 'all of them.'

He is trying to pick them up and looks confused.

Smith knows Shane well. This isn't a try on, it's real and it is serious.

It gets worse; Shane becomes convinced that his food is being poisoned.

His paranoia is growing.

Andy Smith finds an answer to the food problem. He carries a spoon in his back pocket. Every time that Shane is convinced the food has been tampered with, he whips out the spoon and becomes his personal food taster.

'There you go, Shane. I've just had a bit, your turn.'

Shane watches him and once he is sure that he isn't going to drop to the floor writhing in agony, he eats the rest.

Andy talks about him to his governor.

'I have this rapport with him which works well and can de-escalate some situations but he is a dangerous individual. You never turn your back on him, never.'

*

Just how long should a mentally ill inmate stay in solitary confinement?

He has been there for five months because of the hostage situation. He should be there much longer but how much damage will be done if he is kept in solitary for further time?

The prison governor decides to act and, at the end of six months, much to everyone's astonishment, Shane is released back to the wing. At the same time Rob is too.

With hindsight the compassionate decision was a dreadful mistake.

RIOT

Rob had been placed in segregation for an assessment of his mental health issues. They wanted to look at him carefully before they put him on a wing. That tells you something. Rob is reluctant to talk about the offences that led to his imprisonment. It becomes clear that he is bi-polar and has huge mood swings.

Today Rob is very anxious; he knows that other inmates are talking about him. As he passes a group, they stop talking and just watch him 'til he has gone. It's like reading the weather. Some days you can see clouds and it's OK, it is just going to be an overcast day, but there are times when you know the storm clouds are going to burst.

He is scared of going to the showers, scared that a shiv will be pushed into him 'til he feels it deep inside, tearing him apart. Rob is scared of being caught in his cell with someone blocking the door while he is kicked around.

He stands in the dining area and sees one of the lads he is worried about waiting in the queue. There is no mistake, he is glaring and it feels like this is going to be the storm burst. Shane walks past Rob and goes up to the man who had being giving Rob the evil eye. Shane just stands between the two of them and doesn't say a word, his face blank. The other man takes two steps back and it's over. No more problems, just a look that says everything. Rob is under the protection of Shane.

Shane has that status. People know that not only is he a fighter who will take on anybody but also a man who can explode for any reason. You don't mess with lunatics. Shane is popular, everyone likes him, and no one wants to be on the wrong side of him, they call him the 'real deal'.

If Shane knew he was back on the wing early he didn't show any gratitude; he is burning with a deep hatred of the prison system and all those working for it, and will do anything to get back at it. At the heart of his hatred is a belief that they had belittled him, that they didn't show sufficient respect. It also meant that any other inmate who disrespected him was in for a beating.

Shane loves the gym, he works out constantly and has a sculptured body created by steroids and sweat. When the time comes for activities in the prison, officers shout out at the end of the landing. The inmates must then press their buzzers in response if they want to go. Today Prison Officer Eric Lawson shouts out, 'Gym.'

The buzzers can be heard and then he then comes around and opens people's doors. They then go on a movement to leave the wing and arrive at the gym area. Everyone on a movement has to be on a list, whether education, work or other pastimes.

Shane is pressing the buzzer but his door doesn't

open. When eventually Lawson arrives, all the others have gone.

Shane is livid. 'How come you didn't let me out for the gym?'

Lawson says, 'I'll make sure I let you out next time.'

The next day Shane presses his buzzer but the officer doesn't even come on his landing.

'Nah,' he thinks, 'I'm not having this. He's deliberately taking the mick, he's deliberately doing this.'

He presses his buzzer and the guard comes back.

'Why didn't you let me go to the gym?'

He goes, 'Oh. Hmmmmm.'

He is winding Shane up.

'I'm going to do you. You're dead.'

Officer Lawson is not impressed.

'Oh whatever. I've heard it all before. Hmmmmm.'

Shane boots the door and says again,

'I'm going to get you.'

Over lunch when Shane tells the other inmates what has happened, they look at each other. They know if he says, 'I'm going to get you,' then he's going do that. It's just a matter of time.

The purpose of repeating the threat in front of his mates and letting them know his plans is to tie himself in. There is only one question.

'So when's that going to happen?'

A few days later, Shane goes out on association. That's where all the inmates gather together, play pool, watch telly, have a shower, go to the gym, all the free- time stuff. The first person Shane goes to is Rob; after all, Rob owes him. He nods to the square box in the middle of the cross-shaped structure, it houses all the guards. Inside the square box is the office and also it's how everyone gets in and out of the wing. The officers tend to sit near the gates during association time. If anything big kicks off, they can get straight off the wing and lock it off.

'I need to have a distraction, mate.'

Rob was having a down day and was not very keen.

'I dunno, Shane, I don't really want more trouble.'

'Hey, these are the people that put you on seg to assess you but dumped you there and did nothing.' Shane looks him in the eyes. 'And I've helped you.'

'Aye, true you have. Okay then, what do you want me to do?'

The two men start to whisper as Shane sets out his plan.

Later Shane finds some other willing helpers.

The day dawns. Rob has walked past Shane's cell, his eyes are bright and sparkly, and he looks as if he is on speed. It is clearly an 'up' day. Free association is well under way. Shane doesn't buzz for the chance to go to the gym and Eric Lawson doesn't seem to pick up on it.

Showers are important in prison; you are wearing clothes that don't get washed as often as at home and there is a smell in prison that permeates everything. It is a smell of sweat, grime, boiled cabbage and a tang of something underlying it all, bad drains mixed with something worse. Showers give you a chance to feel clean; at least for a while. They are also risky places; every prison novel has a scene where someone is knifed in the showers. Shane isn't scared of any of that; he strides down the landing, towel under his arm. Inside the bundle he is carrying a very large, empty, glass jar of coffee. You buy food and provisions from the canteen and at this point they still sold things in jars.

On each wing there are three floors, Shane is on the second floor and goes down the stairs. Below him next to the stairwell in the middle of the ground floor is a pool table and as usual it is very busy. Rob is there, looking like he is waiting for a game, as if that will ever happen, the winner stays on and the queue is long. Nevertheless he is there looking at every angle of possibility on the table and the best available shots. He hops from foot to foot. Behind him is the gate to the wing from the central area. Officers are spread across the central and wing areas.

Shane holds back but looks towards an older, large, bald and bearded man leaning against the bars. He looks like he would be a biker outside but there are no leathers in here, just a mass of blue sweatshirts and jogging bottoms. He looks up to Shane and there is the merest flicker of acknowledgement as he holds his gaze, then looks away. The older man swings around and looks to a man on the other side of the bars in the central area and nods.

Prison Officer Lawson is next to the pool table on the opposite side. The whole scene is relaxed, there is joking around, music playing, a TV on in the background. Shane slows at the bottom of the stairs and stops about four foot from the table.

Rob starts bouncing up and down on the balls of his feet. He is manic. Suddenly he grabs a handful of pool balls and starts throwing them around whooping and hollering at the top of his voice. All the guards look up and start to move. Lawson is nearest and goes to restrain him. He doesn't see Shane use the towel to hold the top of the jar and smash the bottom against the metal corner of the pool table pocket. It fractures, leaving jagged edges.

Lawson is now moving past Shane towards Rob as the jar lashes out in a slashing, scything motion. The glass catches him in his neck. Only split seconds have passed, the alarm is sounding; guards are starting to sprint towards the wing. The large bearded man closes the gate to the wing and leans his weight into it along with two other men. A number of inmates stand in the way of the guards trying to get past them to the gate from the central area. Lawson is on his own. Shane is thumping him with one hand and stabbing him in the neck and chest with the jar in the other. Blood is spurting everywhere. Rob is still dancing around and throwing balls at anyone and everyone.

Prison Officer Alan Colledge manages to push his way through the gate, but it slams shut after him. He grabs at Shane, who leaves off Lawson and starts to stab his new attacker. A red mist has descended over Shane, he feels pain in his hands; he is cutting himself as well as the guards. Colledge is desperately trying to defend himself, bringing his leg up to defend his groin, but the glass cuts into the back of his thigh, comes out then back again and again and again. There is screaming all around, the noise is incredible. Shane can hear his own heartbeat throbbing in his ears, his vision distorted in time with his thudding pulse.

Others have managed to get in through the gate; batons rain down, fists thump in, kicks hammer into him. The noise gets louder and fuzzier, he turns away from his two victims, covered from head to toe with blood and he sees Rob being folded up like a deckchair and being carried out. He turns back to the guards and the host of faces in front of him, faces twisted in hate and pain, faces of guards he has joked with in the past. All of them are desperate to put him down on the ground.

He is passing out but before the darkness takes him as he falls he sees that he is bleeding and covered with blood too.

The consequences are immediate. The two injured guards, Prison Officer Eric Lawson and Prison Officer Alan Colledge, are rushed to hospital: their fate is up in the air at this point.

Andy Smith hears the news, he is friends with Alan Colledge and when he hears that his colleague has been stabbed he feels physically sick. He isn't surprised to learn it was Shane, he knows him to be an evil individual; there was no other word he can use.

Shane gets carried out bleeding and beaten and is dumped in a special room in segregation called the 'Box'. There are no windows, it is freezing cold and Shane is stripped off naked. There's no bed. No mattress. No blanket. There is a little concrete platform, very narrow, that you might try to use as a bed, but there is no advantage in sleeping on the floor. There is a small cardboard box to use as a toilet. It is 24 hours before he is assessed for his injuries, which will become a problem for the prison.

The prison officers have significant injuries but it turns out that their lives are not in danger from their wounds. Shane has big injuries with a severe gash across his arm and it serves him well. When he goes to court no one can explain where his injuries have come from. His barrister stands up and says,

'Your Honour, Mr Taylor's injuries were quite as bad as those suffered by the officers. In fact the perpetrators would be subjected to the very same charges as those brought before the defendant today.'

The judge listens to what he says and thinks hard.

'I will take into account what you've just said. Mr Taylor does have injuries that would amount to a Section Eighteen charge,' and he added, 'no one's explaining or telling us where these come from.'

He looks over his glasses at Shane standing in the dock.

'I had eight years set in my mind. But I am going cut that down to four years because of what I've just heard.'

So his original sentence for four years and nine months for what were essentially two charges of attempted murder were only extended by another four years for what was also two more attempted murders. The barrister did his job. Shane got off very lightly indeed. A total eight years nine months sentence for stabbing and trying to kill four men.

The prison is in shock after the incident. As a result the men are kept longer in their cells as the regime tries to clamp down on those who have helped Shane and to make sure it doesn't happen again. Two weeks later the BBC reported on the national news that Holme House was in the middle of a three-day prison riot. The prisoners turned violent after being locked up for longer periods, officially described to the press as being because of 'staff shortages'. There is widespread damage to the cells and wing blocks in the incident. The staff and the governor blame Shane despite the fact that he is in the 'Box' downstairs.

The number one governor is relieved of his duties. A guard appears downstairs and tells Shane, 'You are the one who got the governor sacked.'

Rob is carried off to segregation and spends three weeks down there 'til they ship him off to Walton in Liverpool. It is recognised that his bi-polar illness has not been properly diagnosed or appropriately medicated. After further assessment he is sent to Rampton Secure Hospital, one of the three high security psychiatric hospitals for the criminally insane in England.

He is there for five years before being released. Rob was a model patient while in Rampton, apart from an odd moment when he broke a chair over the head of a team leader. It happened out of the blue and to someone he had been friendly towards. Today he is well adjusted and lives in the community.

As long as he takes his medication, he is fine.

DURHAM

Shane is now being moved and is transferred into Durham Prison. Prison officers are only human and we can imagine how they feel. They know that Shane has stabbed two of their colleagues. It is natural for people to react in two different ways in such situations. The first is that 'if I was there, I wouldn't have let him get me.' In other words; an inbuilt macho belief that you are better, stronger and wiser than those who were attacked. The other response is to get revenge, often in small ways; we are not talking about movie-style violence but the small petty and constant ways in which a prisoner can be abused.

They constantly wind Shane up. The lights get flicked on as a guard passes in the middle of the night. His sleep is constantly disturbed. They put him on basic; there is nothing in his cell. They constantly try to get him to lose his temper so that they can come in with truncheons and batons. One of the officers comes to the door,

'Ah, you've got nowt in your cell now. Where are your weapons now, eh?'

Stupid, minor and constant irritations, but Shane has one thing on his side, time.

He thinks, 'Alright then.'

When you have 23 hours in your cell each day, you've got a lot of thinking time.

He lies on his bed looking at the ceiling and the lights. They are heavy industrial units, designed to do their job and be tamper proof. They have big, metal, over-engineered housings, and particular types of screws that you're not meant to be able to get out. Shane discovers that, after many days of working away 23 hours per day, he can get one screw out. Then eventually after many such days he can take off the metal housing. Then he had a formidable weapon.

When they come into Shane's cell, they don't come alone. There are around ten guards coming to Shane to take him out for his legal hour of exercise in the yard.

He waits until the door opens then shouts, 'Boo.'

They all jump back and then form in a half circle outside the door in various fighting positions. Shane takes the metal bar out from behind his back and sees the fear in their eyes. Someone will get seriously injured when it all kicks off. Some brave soul will go first; they will get hit while the others pile in. They are all thinking how many will get taken down before he is under control. They know this is their job and they are up for it, but no one really wants to be first.

Shane holds the thick metal casing out to them.

'Here.'

No one moves. They are all looking at each other

for someone to take the lead.

'Well, you get it then?'

Still no one moves.

'Let me tell you,' he says ,'you can get it, because if I was going to do something, I'd have caved your skull in with it first and you wouldn't have known anything about it. This is a warning. Just get it.'

Finally one of the officers comes slowly forward and takes it from Shane's hands. Shane hangs on to his end for a moment then releases it.

'That's a warning,' he says, 'next time you won't get the warning. I'll cave your skull in.'

He slams the door on them and lies down on his bunk.

Everyone who had previously thought they were too strong and too clever to make a mistake with Shane now understands the threat he poses. Within an hour, literally an hour, a Cat A van arrives and ships him straight to Frankland Maximum Security Prison.

MAX

Frankland, Full Sutton, Long Lartin, Whitemoor and Wakefield are the top security dispersal prisons. Once sent there you only stay within the circuit of maximum security prisons. They don't like to let you settle. If you stay in one place you might get to bond with other serious criminals and the worst of the worst reside in these places. Terrorists, serial killers, and violent rapists: some will never see the light of day outside of prison. They will get old; they will become pale and grey, take on that particular prison pallor. Some will lie in hospital prison beds riddled with cancer, and still never leave, not for punishment's sake, but because they will never be safe, whatever their age and state of health. They will die in prison.

So Shane finds himself at the age of 22 yet again moving into a different league.

The governor at Frankland refuses to put him on the wing where all the other inmates go to socialise; instead Shane is isolated from the off. Normally prisoners are just placed in seg for a disciplinary reason but with Shane the prisons are using it pro-actively and it is long term. Now every time Shane needs to be moved it is with seven prison officers in full riot gear complete with shields. They will not come up to his door without them. He has no television and no books; he is just alone, truly alone.

For Shane it is a blur, days to weeks, weeks to months, and months to years. Alone. His way of coping is to fantasise, his chosen themes are about killing. He again plays the scenes in his head that he has watched so many times on his old video player. He sits planning the destruction of everything around him.

The lights in his cell flash on and off during his sleep. He doesn't get his legal rights to a shower for weeks at a time. The officers often find themselves short handed and unable to let him out for exercise. It may surprise some that this small loss of privilege can have such a major impact on the life of someone in solitary, and already suffering from mental health problems.

A guard boots the door as he walks past; the food when it is delivered has frothy sputum lying on the top of his virtually inedible meal. He believes it is poisoned, he believes they are out to kill him and hatred stacks up, taking up all the space in his head in the tiny cell. The only voices he hears are the ones in his imagination. They sound like Robert de Niro and Joe Pesci. They talk of knives and guns, they talk of punishment, they talk of killing.

*

Eventually Shane is moved to another of the

187

dispersal prisons and he finds himself at Whitemoor. Not every governor will put him in solitary in the seg, some give him a chance and here Shane gets the chance to be on the wing with other prisoners, which is an opportunity to network and do a bit of business.

The bogphone is the only way of passing drugs in and out your cell. Use the string you have made from the threads from the mattress, tangle it with the next cellmate's string and pull drugs through the crusty pipes full of crap. What comes out will be a balloon or cling film wrap, packed with drugs, usually from someone due to leave the seg. Only prisoners about to get a new source of drugs would leave their own stash behind or let someone else have it.

The drugs have been stored in a wrap and pushed up someone's bum to avoid searches. Of course these searches don't happen in the seg because it is 'impossible' apparently for prisoners to pass things to each other. Now stop and wonder how long a balloon or Clingfilm wrap remains intact after repeated insertions and imagine just what state the drugs are in by the time they are hauled through the drains. Prisoners will of course then shove them up their own backsides when they need to, such as when let out for the exercise yard. You don't leave anything in your cell that the guards might find in a search. For the record, the up and coming trend was for a Clingfilm-wrapped plastic Kinder egg tub to be 'cheeked' between the buttocks, rather than full insertion or 'plugged'. Having a plug was to be avoided, if possible, as it could get stuck until nature pushed it back out.

Desperate people do things they wouldn't and probably couldn't imagine in their life before prison. The impact on health is unmeasured because it isn't acknowledged.

For the first time Shane decides to play it smarter. He starts studying the law, using the Archbold books in the library. Guards hate that because he is getting a bit clued on what they can and can't do, or rather what they shouldn't do to him.

Later, when he is left in seg for months on end, he starts making legal complaints about what shouldn't be happening. Often Shane would be on the wing for a month or so, then dragged back on the seg again, because the tension between the guards and him is so bad, fights are commonplace.

It was while he was in Whitemoor that a typical 'non-incident' became inflamed between Shane and a prison officer. Shane has woken with a sore head and is shambling off to breakfast.

A prison officer walks past him and says, 'Are you alright?'

Shane doesn't hear him and trundles off to the serving hatch.

The next thing he knows, there are 20 or so prison officers outside the door of his cell. Shane instantly is up for the fight.

'Alright. Come on, let's go.'

He is pacing up and down the cell, flexing his muscles and bouncing on his toes ready for the kick off. They pile into the cell. The guard who Shane hadn't heard earlier that day is there and comes face to face with him. The guard yells,

'What's your problem with me.'

Shane is confused. 'What are you yelling about? '

'I tried to speak to you earlier on, you didn't speak to me. Are you alright with me? '

'What do you mean?'

'You know what I mean?'

'I didn't hear you. Do you know what I mean?'

The guard is off balance; they had come for a fight. 'Oh, are you sure?'

Shane had been amused but is now losing patience. 'Listen, I'm not being funny. There wasn't a problem, but you're sort of making one right now, you're creating a problem now. Get on your bike, you know. Go away.'

The guard starts to bluster about why Shane hadn't answered him with a 'Good Morning'.

Shane leans into his space until his nose almost touches the startled guard's face.

'Look, you're making a problem here, right now. No, I've got no problem with you but then you come in here like this, you know.'

Now all the tension is back, the guards get panicky. Everything could explode. The guard nods and turns around, the other guards let him through and leave together.

Another day a different prison, Full Sutton or

Wakefield, for Shane the years slip by, memory gets tricky. One of the stories that spreads around the prison system about Shane starts like this. Something has happened, some perceived threat has been raised without Shane being aware of it. He is playing his music with his headphones on. Outside everything is building to a major incident. The inmate in the next cell has looked outside and spotted the guards assembling. He bangs on the walls to warn Shane. The door is closed, and the guards knock to tell him they are coming in as per protocol.

The hammering on the wall eventually gets through to him; he sits up off the bed and pulls off his headphones. The lad is shouting, 'They are coming for you, Shane.'

He looks up and sees the officers through the open hatch in the door, he stands, strips off down to his boxers, the shoes he leaves on (kicks hurt more, and you don't want them stamping on your toes), then stands with his back to the wall opposite to the door. As soon as the six or seven guards come in, he charges at them, bang, he fights them. It lasts for ages, for about 15 to 20 minutes. It becomes talked about through the prison very quickly, the incredible wildfire of whispers and shouts from the landings. Within an hour the stories say the fight lasted three quarters of an hour.

When you're getting roughed up by guards in riot gear and it's lasting that long, it gets respect throughout the system.

Shane was later to arrive at other prisons and find

that the story had gone the rounds; once an inmate is transferred their stories of derring-do go with them. They tell others, they move, and suddenly the whole prison system gets to know about the gossip.

It spread all around the maximum-security prisons.

'He's off his head man. It took them about forty minutes to pin him down.'

The reality is that it was brutal and since Shane was in his shoes and boxers and the guards were in full riot gear Shane was the one who was damaged and it was back to the seg.

He decides to be awkward, there is walking and there is being 'twisted open', essentially both arms twisted up 'til your head is down below your elbows.

They tell him to stand and walk, he doesn't, so they 'twist him open'. He still doesn't walk despite the fact that they can more or less force him forward; he flops off the floor instead and shouts, 'You'll have to carry me.'

They have a walk of about a mile to the other end of the prison wing.

'Get up.'

'No, just carry me.'

The guards are furious; many of them are hurt despite their body armour.

'Well, you know what we'll do. We'll ram every door with your head.'

'You better use me head then.'

They carry him head first and they do hit every door

and doorpost along the way. Every bash becomes a badge of honour. Shane is literally a head case.

At one time Shane is banned from buying certain things from the canteen. Baby oil, shampoo and butter. It seems like an odd mix and an entirely random decision. However even Shane agrees that they were in the right.

Things were tense on the wing. Shane had come out of the seg and the prison officers and management were waiting for the next round of trouble. The guards were constantly looking into his room dreading seeing him stripped down to his boxers and boots. It was his way of saying, 'Hello do you want to have a fight?'

Of course the day came. The hatch is opened and there is Shane suddenly shouting the odds. There is a buzz around the wing, inmates rush to their doors trying to see what happens through the cracks. The hatches are designed so you can't see a thing, but people always want to try. Besides it is an act of solidarity to stand with your ear to the door and try to picture what is going on. Suddenly there is the sound of running feet. The officers are in riot gear and tooled up with shields and batons.

There are cries of 'Give'em hell, Shane', and other more lurid encouraging shouts of support. As things stand, on the grand scorecard of prison league fights, Shane has only had the slightest of victories, the best he can hope for is that he survives. He can only hope to damage the pride of the guards by the length of the fight. Still he sounds well up for this rematch.

The sounds get louder. Not being able to see out of the locked cells means that everyone must imagine the scene before them, the clues lie in the screams, grunts and groans of the participants. Then there are the sounds a baton makes when it hits soft flesh and the way a boot smacks into the side of someone lying down.

So get yourself comfortable and imagine you are there.

First the preamble. Shane shouts his challenges. The call and then the response. There is the alarm, the sound of running feet. Then a pause, guards are assembling. It all takes longer than it should but maybe it just seems so because you are standing waiting. If the guards are really up for a scrap they might do that tribal thing, they always seem to nick from foreign rugby teams. There is the ritual smacking of the baton on the shield. They are psyching themselves up, getting into battle mode, readying and making their own threat of intimidation. Except these aren't real warriors, they are civil servants in riot gear who don't want to fight. Probably one of them is busy pooing himself as he wonders, 'Is it going to be me today?'

Shane in the background is keeping up his own mantra of swearing and threats, at times loud enough to be heard properly, at other times at a lower volume, about what he is going to do to them.

Then the phony war ends.

The door can be heard to bang open. Then unexpectedly there are screams, and it's not Shane.

People are cursing, shouting, there are slapping sounds, falling. A short while later, there are cries of:

'He's a slippery sod.'

'Hold on to him.'

'I can't.'

'Arggh.'

It goes on for a while.

The screaming and cries of pain are clearly only coming from the guards.

Shane is laughing like a maniac.

Eventually, there is the sound of the cell door slamming shut, and the sound of guards cursing and moaning fades into the distance. All that is left is Shane giggling and shouting for them to come back. Unexpectedly the scorecards are clearly marked down as a win for the wing.

Shane ten, guards zero.

What they couldn't understand is how.

If the inmates could have seen what was happening rather than just listen to it from behind their cells doors they would have discovered this.

The first prison guards ran into the cell then slipped straight on to their backsides on the floor, skidded hard across the cell, then smacked into the wall. Shane then treated them to some well placed kicks into exposed tender areas that were no longer protected by their shields.

There was total confusion, the next guards in

slipped and fell too, until someone twigged that the floor was coated with shampoo and butter and utterly impossible to walk on and remain upright. The whole cell with the exception of the small area where Shane was standing was covered. Some of them slithered across the floor to grab him, but then found that he was coated head to toe in baby oil and impossible to hold. The remaining guards who had not come into the cell were trying to grab and pull back their fallen comrades. The ones who were left on the floor were suffering from Shane's attacks. He had managed to pick up a shield and now he was using it on them. Battered and bruised, all of the guards were eventually pulled out and the door locked again.

*

For all the stories of what appears to be a brutally controlling regime, Shane offers up no real criticism of the prison guards or even the governors. They operate in a world that is hard for outsiders to see and understand. Segregation with its impact on fragile mental health is clearly near the top of the list of things that need to be addressed, as does the design of prisons. Governors operate within the framework provided for them. Guards, by definition, have to control the most violent, manipulative and dangerous people in our society. Prison guards themselves fall into at least two camps, those for whom it is a calling of sorts, who see their role as providing correction and rehabilitation within a controlled setting. Then there are those for whom it is a job. Both types of officers have good and bad examples. It is possible just to see it as a job but be incredibly professional in what you do. Some with 'vocations' have proved to be inept.

Some guards are young and may not have gained sufficient experience to be able to rise above provocation. The point is that in these very human conditions, violence and lies surround guards and inmates alike. For those who pontificate that prison is like a holiday camp, they have no idea at all, unless their idea of a holiday involves mental torture, physical harm, stress and the most unsanitary practices possible.

The underground network of gossip runs not only among prisoners but also the Prison Service. Shane is known wherever he goes and so there is an instant dislike between him and the guards in each new prison. They have read his file, they have talked to colleagues, they expect trouble and they get it. When, inevitably, Shane kicks off, he will find himself not just in a prison, but a prison in a prison, not just on seg, but in seg on a specialist segregation unit. The CSC.

TWENTY SIX

2004

CSC

It all comes to a head while Shane is in the segregation unit inside a maximum security prison. There is an established protocol imposed on him which is designed to protect the officers. Shane has to be seen through the hatch to be standing at the back wall facing away from the door, with his hands on his head. The door then slams open, and a shield appears at the end of the doorway. On hearing this Shane has to walk back, hands still on his head, as slowly as he can. As soon as his back touches the shield of the front guard, he then puts his hands behind his back and has to step back again until his hands touch the shields of the next two guards behind the lead officer.

'Step to the side... now back...'

They then push him forward with their shields and the next four guards enter with their shields right behind their colleagues, until he is face into the wall with a phalanx of guards pushing him forward. His face is cold against the breeze-block wall.

'Hands.'

He holds one arm out against the wall, then the other. As he does so, an officer grabs the arm with both hands, the same on the other side. Shane's face is now squashed against the wall, a shield pressed into his back. The force of all the other guards press against him. His arms are outstretched and are held in place against the breeze-blocks by officers on each side. All the guards are in full armour and full riot gear.

Now he is ready to be searched. When that happens everything is searched, seams of the clothes, hair, ears, mouth, nostrils and then the other places too.

'Go to the next cell, we're going to search you.'

As he stands there something about it all doesn't feel right and he becomes fully alert. He is tight against the wall, moving an inch at a time to his right, flush against the wall until he leaves the cell and is pushed into the next one. At last he finds himself pressed up to the window with his hands on either side of the frame. He realises that it is all taking too long, that something is going on behind his back. He turns but is smashed in his face with the shield.

Two prison officers grab each hand but, rather than resist, he slides his hands down the wall; it is in an instant, quick as a flash, and a guard overbalances and falls. Shane forces himself away from the wall, bends down and tries to pick him up by the leg. As the guards heave forward, Shane falls and drops on top of the guard. Shane pushes his own legs back against the wall and manages to get into the middle of the cell taking the guard with him, then pushes into the corner, caught up between the toilet and the wall. The guard has a riot helmet on, but his eyes go wide with fear as he looks directly into Shane's as he comes close to the Perspex mask. The problem for the guard is that his shield, which is on the floor, traps his arms, and others are standing on it. He cannot get his arm out of the holding loop. His other hand is pinned down under the boot of another guard.

The guard is now panicking. Shane, all six foot six of muscle, is on top of him and has managed to free his arms. The other officers are panicking as well. Shane, however, is focused and trying to get his hands under the face mask of the guard to get to his throat. He is nutting the face mask, spitting at it, trying everything he can to produce terror in the guard. The others are kicking at Shane, pulling his hair, which is difficult given his short cut. Shields bounce off him, batons come down but only some of them hit him, others hit their own colleagues in the melee.

Shane never stops staring directly into the panicking guard's eyes, his hands are digging under the mask and the guard is doing everything he can to force his head up off the ground to stop him.

Shane growls,

'Dude, if I get your neck today, you're not going home. You're dead.'

The guard squeals in terror, he is gurgling in fear, he is wetting himself and in near shutdown.

One of Shane's hands gets under the mask and he goes to get his hand around the guard's neck.

Just then a baton hammers his arm until the muscle loses its power and it is dragged back.

The tide has turned and more of the guards are in a

position to attack. Shane somehow appears to be able to switch off; not reacting to pain that would stop others. He lies there as they drag the fallen guard away and turn to stamp, punch, kick and beat him non-stop.

His hands are handcuffed and a guard jumps in with his hands to Shane's throat. He squeezes his windpipe until he turns blue in the face, relaxes until Shane exhales, then squeezes again.

'You coward.'

He sees Shane go purple and relaxes, and at first he thinks Shane is crying but then to his fury he realises that he isn't, he's laughing. The choking starts up again until the guard is dragged off by those who think that it might go on too far.

'Seven of you bastards against one man and you call me a coward.'

He laughs again and the kicking starts.

Later the care manager arrives. She is tasked to hear complaints from the prisoners. Shane is sitting with the side of his face ballooned up in a mass of purple swellings and cuts.

'Is everything alright?'

'Yeah, fine thanks.'

She does a double take.

'You're okay…?'

'Yeah, you?'

Shane is deciding to wind them up by ignoring what has happened. The reason is that he has gone the other route often enough. A woman doctor once visited him after a beating by some prison officers. He detailed each injury as she took notes.

When eventually he got to see the report, none of his injuries were mentioned, everything she wrote down was a lie.

As Shane says, 'Sack it'.

Speaking about it to a friend he says, 'I realised it was pointless. Who is gonna listen to this person that was a schizophrenic mentally ill nutcase, who's got a violent record longer than his arm, or a couple of nice prison guards. I know who people gonna listen to.'

The outcome of the fight: handcuffs on, leg irons on, and he is shipped out again to yet another prison. Unbeknownst to Shane wheels are in motion. The Home Office have received reports from all the governors where he has served parts of his sentence. The reports are collated and assessments undertaken. Every one points to the fact that Shane is a killer 'in waiting'. Once you serve a proportion of your sentence you are assessed to see if you qualify for any form of early release. The Prison Service is sure that he should not have any part of his sentence commuted; furthermore he is classed as one of the six most dangerous prisoners in the whole of the English penal system. This time it is not just a new prison, it is inside a maximum security prison, inside their segregation unit where there lies a 'close supervision centre' cell. This was a special one-off CSC, rather than the bigger CSC units.

Prison rule 46 allows for prisoners to be held in a CSC. These are small units or individually designed cells within some of the Category A prisons. Its aim is to remove the most disruptive, challenging and dangerous prisoners from their ordinary prison location and manage them within small and highly supervised units. Assessments are carried out as to the prisoner's risk, and supposedly followed by individual and/or group work to try to reduce the risk of harm to others. As their risk reduces, the prisoner can then be returned to a normal or more appropriate location.

Across the board the close supervision centre (CSC) system holds about 60 of the most dangerous men in the prison system in the UK. Many of these are men who have been imprisoned for very serious offences, which have caused great harm. They have usually committed subsequent very serious further offences in prison and their dangerous and disruptive behaviour is too difficult to manage in an ordinary prison. They are held in small units or individual designated cells throughout the high security prison estate. These men are likely to be held for many years in the most restrictive of conditions with limited stimuli and human contact.

A central team as part of the Prison Service's high security directorate runs the system, although day to day management is the responsibility of the individual prisons in which the units or cells are located.

However, prison inspectors, having visited all of the CSCs, reported concerns that 'a minority of managers and staff do not understand the ethos of the system or embrace their role within it. Too often it leads to prisoners being held there for many months or even years, with poor regimes and little emphasis on progression, which is contrary to the prison rule 46 under which they are held'. They concluded the report saying that 'finally more needs to be done to offset the real potential for psychological deterioration' and commented that some cells were 'cramped and unsuitable'.

In practice it is the segregation to the power of two. There is zero human contact. The cells are specially constructed so that the bogphone and other ways of interaction don't work. Zero human contact, no visits, not even a human interaction with a guard. Food comes through a hatch that cannot be opened from the cell until the other side is locked. Staff are searched constantly, no drugs or telephones are smuggled in by staff or available from other inmates.

If Shane's cell door gets opened, there have to be seven specially trained prison officers, riot shields on, riot gear ready because people on CSC are attacking officers constantly. It takes half an hour to an hour just to walk to the exercise cage, a tiny, heavily protected space for one.

Shane's time in CSC was tough. His unit wasn't one where the enlightened approach to rehabilitation was favoured, but rather one of those highlighted by the prison inspectors as being 'where people are left to rot'. Mentally Shane is going down into a deep hole to the worse places possible. He isn't highlighted as someone who needs to be put on suicide watch, which is fortunate. 'Suicide watch' has a ring of compassion about it, but the truth is stark. Everything stays the same apart from the fact that they take your clothes, blankets and mattress from you so you can't hang yourself.

That's it. Now you are in solitary, freezing cold and have no clothes and a bare concrete bench to try to sleep on. And you are still alone.

So no, Shane isn't on suicide watch but they should have realised that he wasn't turning that desperation into self-pity and self-destruction, he was turning it into a plan to kill people who had crossed him. All the time he is here he knows that in a few years they have to let him out because he will have served his time. Then he is going to start to take his vengeance. Even though it may mean his death by the hands of the police or a life spent behind bars, he is going to kill.

PLANS

Although the rain has stopped, the branches overhead are still bowed and heavy. The leaves are brown and just waiting for a moderate breeze that will surely come and strip them from the branches. It is cold and the water drips in large droplets down on to his head and shoulders. A rivulet runs down his face but he waits utterly still, his eyes taking in everything. His sight is so well adjusted now to the dark that he can make out the glass shards from the bulbs in the gutter around the base of the lamppost. He smiles to himself.

'See, Taz can do what he's told.'

The feel of the night air moves around him whispering against the back of his neck. He breathes deeply; he hasn't felt this in years. Being in an exercise yard isn't the same as being really outside, it still feels like prison even when you close your eyes. The presence of the rolls of barbed wire on the top of the fences and the walls of the house-block towering above you stay there, no matter what.

He waits although he doesn't need to, they are all long in bed, but there is a special thrill in just standing here outside so many houses. All those people asleep. All of them unaware of just how vulnerable they are. They have nothing that he can't take, their money, and their valuables, even their very last breath. None of them can stop him, he could break into any one of their houses if he wants, but that's not what he is after. Just a few moments more, and then...

He jogs silently to the other side of the road, past his parked car, and is up and over the high fence. Taz did the recce for him last night after breaking the street lamps with an airgun.

'Three gardens from the side road. First one, no problem, second one, don't jump near the house, they have a tool store right next to the back door, jump three metres further down, third one is fine.'

He vaults the fences, hands up, body swinging to the side, up and over. He stands now in the garden of the house he wants...

Someone bangs on a cell door in the distance. At night sound travels differently. There is the sound of someone crying that falls away into broken sobs, and then it's gone. The prisoner might have stopped or maybe a door has closed. He stares at the blank breeze-block wall as he sits on the bunk bed, his eyes eventually lose their focus, slowly he is back in his fantasy again.

The kitchen window is open slightly but he doubts whether he can fit through it, better to go through the door. He has been breaking into houses since he was six; there isn't much that will stop him. The best most people can do to make their house secure is to make it more difficult than their neighbour's. It's like that old saying about two antelopes running away from a lion. One says, 'Do you really think we can outrun it?' The other replies, 'No, I just need to outrun you.'

But that isn't the case now, it isn't a case of whether he can break in, it's just about how messy it will be. Once in the house he will need to be fast but very quiet. He has waited for an hour after the last light was switched off. After this, in a few hours' time, well before dawn, he will be in the second prison officer's house on his list. He doesn't want the bodies to be discovered until he is off to deal with those others that have grassed him up. They will all be in bed late, lazy sods. Still, he will have all the time he wants to deal with them. For those it will be in and out, do the business and then off again. He picks the lock to the back door and deals with the alarm; he will prepare downstairs in the living room…

Back in the cell he stops to correct himself. Slowly he builds the scene again in his mind's eye. He pauses for thought and then loses himself. If anyone had come into the cell at that point he probably wouldn't have noticed. He builds his imaginary world, every detail, layer upon layer, mentally testing his decision-making and adjusting the plan. It is what he will do as soon as he is released. He is destined to be a lifer, destined to be locked up for life and as long as he can do these killings in this way he will be happy.

He corrects himself; he must do what he plans upstairs.

He is going up the stairs to the bedroom as quiet as a church mouse. His feet are on the outside of each tread where there is less chance of a creak. He stands on the landing and waits. He stands with his mouth open and holds his breath. It is the easiest way to hear properly for any hint of someone waking. He is happy to wait there ten minutes in total silence. If someone has woken they will either do something or drop off back to sleep.

He knows the prison guard is married but has no kids.

He checks the rooms for tell-tale signs.

He has debated the relative merits of a face mask. He doesn't need it, no one in the house will be able to say who it was and, even if they did, it wouldn't matter. They would guess soon enough. He isn't even going to wear gloves or bother about the random hairs or flakes of skin we all discard. No, telegraph it, let them all know from the beginning who it is. As long as he has 24 hours to do what he wants, then it doesn't matter. But still, maybe the mask...

The advantage of wearing it will be about terror and control. He gets both with a mask. Without it, as soon as the guard sees who it is they will know they are dead people.. That might reduce his ability to control everything.

He pauses to think it through, his mind's eye going over every detail he has built up. Inside his head, over the weeks and months, he has created a vast imaginary world. What type of house will a prison guard have on his salary, what sort of wife, what would they choose in carpets, wallpaper, and furniture? He goes back to the control issue.

Control: if he goes in fast while they are asleep and thumps the guard hard, really hard. Would that be best? The wife might try to scream but he could grab her before she was even awake. If the guard is knocked out by the punch, great. If not, he sees wifey with a knife to her throat, a large nine-inch kitchen blade with a deadly gleaming edge. He changes his mind.

He nips the nose of the woman as she lies sleeping, she

gasps for breath but his hand comes over her mouth and he points the knife a mere inch away from her eye, just to focus her mind.

Her husband wakes as she thrashes her legs, only for him to see his wife with the knife to her throat. A starburst sparkle of moonlight runs along the edge of the knife.

The best outcome is played over and over again though he works through all the different scenarios of loss of control. It's all the same in the end of course, but he is determined to enjoy it. Now is the time for the punch, he smashes it into the side of his head, catching him on the temple and cracking his eye socket. Wifey thrashes about, panicking.

Time moves along.

The guard wakes up, tied to the chair, a gag ball strap around his mouth, just like the one in Pulp Fiction. His swollen eye is half closed shut, blood is caked on the side of his face. He wakes with a start, suddenly conscious. He strains against the straps holding him tight to the chair, and then he sees what is before him. He panics, he wants to scream threats, he wants to beg, he wants to offer Shane money, he wants... he wants...

But it is about what Shane wants, and what he wants is revenge, he wants pain, and he wants blood.

The wife is tied to a chair.

For a moment he dwells on the idea of when to bring chairs up from below. Do families nowadays always have chairs in their bedrooms, what is the current fashion? He doesn't know, he has been locked up so long, and before that he never went in for any best British boudoir competitions. He parks it as an idea to resolve later. He has plenty of time to work it out. He can spend weeks on this one detail if he needs to. Play it out in every way possible.

He blinks, stares at the cream-coloured painted breeze-block wall in front of him until it returns him to the images in his head. It is as if the wall dissolves into a paused video screen. It starts to play.

The guard really starts to understand what is happening. Shane has a reel of fishing wire threaded through a needle. He approaches the wife. She screams as she sees it near her face.

He plays the details over and over again, which order would produce the maximum pain for the guard? Yes, definitely to the wife first.

'If you can save you or your wife, which one will it be?'

The guard is desperately trying to get free and scream.

'I know you can't talk, don't worry, I'll help you.'

'Do you want to save wifey?'

'One of you has to go, bonny lad. I'll make it easy for you, I'll start with wifey, unless you stop me.'

He starts his bloody work. Her face is a picture of horror, her lips sewn shut first, and then her nostrils, neither sown tight; she must breathe after all. Lastly the eyes.

'If you don't look, I'll cut off your eyelids.'

He goes over to the guard and peels his lid back between his thumb and fingertip. He pulls it right back, stretching it high above his eyebrow, right to the point of it tearing. The guard's terror overcomes him and he loses control of his bowels. A dark stain spreads across his lap. The smell is vile. He slaps him across his cheek.

'Dirty boy.'

He looks at the clock, it is four o'clock, he is running late. Two prison guards and their wives, then on to the grasses. The informers are already locked up in an old deserted garage at the edge of an old allotment. They can wait; the three of them are tied up, lured after the pubs closed down. A lad offered them a cheap score and took them down with a baseball bat as they came in. Straps, chairs, sitting in a pool of their own piss waiting for him to come back. They can wait.

He is getting to the punchline, the line he has rehearsed over and over again in his mind for the years he has been in solitary.

'Look what you did. Look what you've done, all of this is because of you.'

He stands behind the wife. He isn't a monster; he will put them all out of their misery. His knife does its work; he imagines the spray, a fountain of blood. The guard wants to turn away but cannot, he cannot even see the eyes of his wife to say goodbye because they are sown up shut. The knife finishes her and then he starts on the guard.

Shane comes round. He is still in his cell, he doesn't feel the cold, he doesn't care about the concrete bunk, the tiny room, the absence of another human being, the crap food that comes through the hatch, the twice a week he is manacled out to the exercise cage for his exercise: 20 minutes to get him there, ten minutes exercise – or rather a walk around a cage, and then 20 minutes walk back. He isn't fighting them now with his hands. He fights them in his mind. He talks to himself.

'I don't care if I get caught. I'll die happy knowing I got revenge. I'll get revenge and I'll have peace. They'll never forget me and what they've done to me.'

Whatever he looks like to the guards who are supervising him and to the prison authorities that are supposed to be monitoring him and helping him to address his offending behaviour, what is really going on is that he is looking at them with murder in his heart.

'Look what you did. Look what you've done, all of this is because of you.'

He knows the end of his sentence is coming up in just a couple of years; he just needs to be patient. People misunderstand the word patience. People think it's passive, just another word for waiting. The old way it used to be defined was different. It meant literally to grit your teeth, to battle on, to do what you have to do to keep going.

That's patience, and Shane has it by the bucket load.

Despite Shane being away in CSC and having no contact with anyone, inmates know by some sixth sense that the storm is coming. Maybe a guard talks to a friend and is overheard by a prisoner.

'Shane is no trouble nowadays.'

Those who know him know that isn't how it's going to go, and outside the prison hardened criminals keep reminding themselves of the dates on the calendar and figuring out what they are going to do when the day comes for his release. Shane has 12 people who he plans to murder in cold blood. 12 people who have crossed him and who he will torture and kill before he is arrested or killed by the armed police.

TWENTY EIGHT

2005

DRUGS

The powers that be must have looked at the reports and figured it's worth trying. They are deciding whether to allow Shane back out on the wing. Has he reformed? He hasn't tried to fight his guards for a half a year, and in just under two years he must be released. They don't know that Shane has changed tactics; he doesn't want to fight inside, he wants to be released to be able to kill two particular prison guards and around ten people he feels are sure to have grassed him up.

A normal prisoner would only serve half their time and then the early release scheme cuts in for good behaviour. Well, in Shane's case forget that, but, normally when someone is in their last year, they get reduced Cat classification, 'A's down to 'B's etc. Maximum security inmates go down to 'ordinary' cons prisons. So there is a clear rationale behind the move to try it out, but they need be very careful. If there is the slightest hint of violence; ship him out back to a CSC cell. The guard comes to Shane's pad and stands in the doorway without riot gear; his protection is secretly waiting to the side of the door out of sight.

'Shane, do you want to get out?'

Shane blinks and stands.

'Yes.'

'Have you ever been abroad?'

'No.'

'Well, you're going to today, sunshine.'

Shane is on the ferry to the Isle of Wight, on his way to the famous prison there. Well, when we say on the ferry, he is really handcuffed to a rail, inside a cage, inside a van on the ferry. But he can feel the way the waves are swaying beneath his feet and he is moving around without the certainty of dry and solid land. It is the first time he has been at sea.

When he is on the wing, the authorities are impressed, there is no fighting the guards, there are one or two run-ins with the other prisoners but that is to be expected, pecking orders must be established, some noses put of out joint, often literally.

Shane is bulking up in the gym and starting to sell some heroin with his mate John from Gateshead. His reputation has spread abroad even down here. He is the man who has stabbed two guards, fought off seven riot guards in his cell for 45 minutes; he has nearly killed another riot guard while in the seg. Other lurid stories circulate, a mix of truth, falsehoods and exotic exaggerations. He is looked on as being 'super game', meaning up to hurt anyone by any means; he is seen as being crazy. The kind of person who would not think twice of putting a knife in your neck. The kind of person in prison or out who you don't want turning up at your door. In other words, he is regarded not so much as a rock-hard fighter, but more as a madman, a human time-bomb that could go off without warning. When he explodes you do not want to be caught up in it.

Shane can pull enormous reserves of energy and can block his own pain in a fight, but he lacks the ability to think and stand back, he is a classic 'berserk'. The old 'baresark' Viking warriors would fight without armour, swinging the sword at anything in front of them, friend or foe, until there was no one left standing to kill. Only at that point did they tally up whether they had killed more of their enemies or friends. Maybe Viking genes are to blame after all.

Once introduced to steroids Shane has put on three stones of muscle and he was already a large man to start with. Steroids, however, do not help those with mental illness who have problems controlling their rage. John and Shane start using the money made from selling heroin to get extra canteen purchases and send some money back home to their families. The biggest thing they are after, though, are mobile phones. The prison phones are monitored and, even if you talk in code, you can get caught when organising drug smuggling. Most codes are broken down quite quickly, after all most of the inmates who make them up aren't exactly Bletchley boffins, it's more like, 'Can you drop that thingy we talked about around to Harry's tomorrow and persuade him to do that thing we discussed.'

So if you do want to tell someone to drop off some gear to an address and threaten them until they are willing to bring in the drugs on a visit, you really do need secure lines of communication. Acquire a smuggled mobile phone and then you are in the money.

Everyone has heard of the drug problems in prisons and if people think the problem should be solved with some simple measures then they are misinformed. It is a tough, challenging and almost insurmountable problem.

Before trying to understand the drugs problem it is necessary to try to understand how prisons work in the UK. It is very different to America and very different to how it is portrayed on television and in the movies.

Let's start with your day in court and, for argument's sake, let's presume you are guilty and you know you are going to be sent down. What are the dos and don'ts? When the judge or magistrate passes a custodial sentence, you go straight to prison as you are, so think about what you are wearing. First shoes, make sure they are unbranded, but the most comfortable pair you have, because you are going to be wearing them for a long time. Next don't take in any items that have value unless you are capable of standing up to, and fighting, a bully who decides to relieve you of that nice watch or your posh trainers.

Most of those who know their stuff will take in some things with them when they go to court for sentencing. Remember you leave immediately after being sent down. You are taken from the dock, down the stairs and into the cells to be processed by a guard. What you have with you will follow you.

Here is some more advice. Take underwear, lots of it. Wear it all in one go if you have to but don't go looking like a 'Michelin Man'. Take cash, as much as you can get together and, as mentioned, remember to take in good shoes.

Some say to take some toiletries, as it will save you money later, but not luxury brands, they may not be allowed. Some know they are going to go on to an open prison after reception and take books, stamps, writing paper, pens and pencils, envelopes, and a radio alarm clock. Others think that it is better to have all these things brought in for you on your first visit along with a stereo, CDs and the like. iPods are more difficult; if the prison thinks they can be used for communication they get banned, so better to stay old school. All these things have a low to zero probability however of being allowed in a Cat B nick. Many feel the best advice is don't stress about taking things in – it will just be more stuff to deal with on the day of sentencing and more to go through with the guard.

Passing into reception at the prison, you will be provided with prison issue: bedding, clothes, cutlery, towels, socks, underwear, and toiletries. Some prisons give you a reception pack of baccy, with Rizlas, matches and sweets. You can, if you prefer, opt for a non-smoker's pack. If you are moved to another prison you leave all the prison issue things you were given behind. You will be given a new set in the next prison.

Your cash gets signed in and goes towards your 'canteen'. The canteen is the prison banking and shopping system. Any money you have when you arrive at reception, plus money sent in on your behalf, will be put into your private cash account. Ordinary household items can be bought in the canteen. You can buy phone credit, stamps, writing paper, chocolate, biscuits, cereal and some tinned stuff. It's all things you need, but a basic supermarket economy brand standard and quite cheap.

If you have the money, you are allowed to spend initially about £15 per week plus your 'wages' of about £1 a day if you work or go to education while in prison. It happens automatically – you just need to keep that 'private cash' account topped up sufficiently. Those who know the game try to take in £100 to get through the first month or so, then a postal order from someone on the outside is the most efficient way of topping up.

What you order from the canteen will arrive on a set day each week about four days from ordering. Now think about the opportunity that presents for drugs. Drugs don't have to be what you might expect. Household items first. There are things you buy from the canteen and mix together to get you high. Now start thinking about legally obtained prescription drugs. When medications are used in prison, inmates don't always swallow the pills they receive. Basically they tuck them under their tongue or under their cheek, and get them out later to trade. There is always someone who is 'cheeking' their meds, either to trade or stockpile for getting high. When you make a trade, prescription pills can be swallowed, snorted, or mixed with other drugs.

There a lot of myths about drugs in prison as well. Some stories in circulation may have some roots in the American prison system but not in the UK.

It is said that some make 'crack sticks' by crushing up a filter from an electronic cigarette, coating it with a type of pain reliever, and smoking it. Others smoke paper that has been saturated with coffee – a practice known as 'parachuting' – though you may well fail to see how paper soaked in coffee can get you high. One suggested use for pills is 'whippit', a potent, taffy-like concoction made from melted candy and coffee, combined with drugs used for treating depression and bi-polar disorder. It is said to be very addictive. Shane has never come across it and is scathing.

'I can't see how coffee and candy could make any difference to me just popping the tablets.'

There are some hilarious stories in circulation; apparently one man was arrested after methadone-soaked underwear was smuggled in. It was only when guards wondered why other inmates were chewing pieces of his underpants that they got suspicious. However since doctors give methadone freely to addicts, it is very unlikely to have happened. Another urban myth is about bringing in a book with you when you leave court. Pages can be pre-soaked in liquid suboxone, a substance used to treat heroin addiction; even heroin can be smuggled in that way. It's all just a nonsense of course, and not worth the effort. Drugs are so freely available and cheap, why on earth would you bother.

Smuggling routes are not particularly challenging

and easy to do. If they did a drugs raid on the queue of people waiting to come in for a prison visit, they would have nearly all of them in court on charges. Even the kids are at it, though maybe their mums are to blame. It has stopped now but once a baby's nappies were a good way to bring in drugs, especially a dirty nappy. Guards don't want to wade through all that brown stuff, and mum just needs to insert the Clingfilm-wrapped drugs into the middle of a squashed up pile of turds. It is easy, the inmates can wash it off in the bathroom before they unpack and use it. Nowadays all nappies worn by babies must be replaced with prison-stock disposable nappies before the guests are searched and go in to meet their better halves in the visitors' room. So that route has stopped.

The point is that, whatever the prison system does to stop drugs, the inventiveness of people to find ways of using even legitimately purchased items, will always open up unforeseen ways of getting or trying to get high. Smuggling is constantly finding new ways for drugs to be brought in. Legal highs have made their way into the prisons; some, like the artificial synthetic marijuana drug Spice, are very potent. Heroin, steroids, grass, resin, uppers, downers, speed, meth, and cocaine are everywhere, although some external events govern their desirability and prevalence.

The war on drugs always has unforeseen consequences. Drug testing sounds like a good idea, doesn't it? However, the Prison Service shot itself in the foot when it brought in random testing. They needed to lessen drug use in prison so they decided to test both randomly and frequently. The punishment for having been caught with drugs in your bloodstream was more prison. Suddenly they were nicking a load of inmates for smoking weed and the prisoners were losing days off their remission. Overnight all the people who were smoking cannabis switched to heroin because cannabis stays in the bloodstream far longer than other drugs, so they switched from the relatively less harmful cannabis to heroin because it leaves the body fast and is very difficult to detect.

The governor can add days to an inmate's stay in prison but not extend their actual original sentence. So someone who is due to serve half their sentence of, say, 18 months would expect release under licence in nine months. However, the governor can add time beyond the release date on the nine months but cannot extend it past the original 18 month sentence. Each extension is dealt with by a 'mini trial' in the prison itself. For serious offences like stabbing, the prisoner goes back to the courts and new sentences may be added on.

The simple truth is that drugs are all over prison and prisoners can get drugs easier than on the outside. Shane sees a lot of people who had never taken heroin before they were put in prison, come in, use it, serve their sentences and leave as heroin addicts.

The primary routes are corrupt officers, closely followed by inmates' visitors. Any inmate going to court will also be likely to bring drugs back with them, plugged up their bums.

Let's also deal with the myths about how it is all organised. The easy answer is that, by and large, it isn't. There are no John Gotti types of characters organising things. Although, on one hand, prison is full of nutters, hard men, all from different areas, with a pride-based machismo that dominates with a 'never backing down mentality', prison is also run through people trying to get on and do favours.

In one prison a few lads were getting their friends to throw weighted packages tied to a long string, which would be hurled over the prison wall once enough momentum had been gained by swinging them round and round. The red-band prisoners are trusted inmates who work as cleaners and can go anywhere in the prison. Shane would ask them to pick up the packages as they went around the inner walls gathering rubbish. They would come back to Shane, who then gave them a cut to take or sell on. Sometimes instead Shane and his mate John would buy drugs from the red-bands and organise payment to be sent to their nominated addresses.

Favours, cash, that's how it works. No big cheese, no threats, no organisation, just everyone at it as a way of getting by. However, as stated, the biggest route is via corrupt officers.

There are all sorts of accounts of different schemes that have been uncovered, and some officers have found themselves prosecuted and sent to the very cells they used to guard. In one of the top security prisons even canteen staff have been corrupted. In some cases Weetabix boxes and protein powder tubs have been emptied of their rightful contents, re-filled with drugs, and then resealed. Other ideas and methods are endless: one scheme involved a bent officer based in the canteen who put his own special packets of Pot Noodles on the shelves. He even bought a proper machine matching the one in the Pot Noodle factory to re-seal them. After all, as long as the seal is unbroken no one is going to pick up on it. The stock had to be coded with tiny pen marks and given to the right people. The officer was paid to do it by some kind folks outside the prison. The guard wasn't caught and might still be in his retirement villa even now, enjoying the sun. Many of these accounts derive not from Shane but from the Home Office's own reports into drug smuggling.

After the corrupt officers, it is the visits themselves that account for the huge amounts brought in. The conventional route for smuggling phones and drugs into the prison are usually Clingfilm wrap or Kinder Eggs with contraband inserted into the body cavities. Watch out for visitors who limp and look cross-eyed. They are the greedy ones.

The most common route for smuggling is for someone to approach a druggie inmate. They set them up to receive a stream of visitors, each of whom will carry in drugs. The visitor may be carrying the drugs in a wrap held between the buttocks, but if strip-searched and made to squat it is touch and go as to whether it will drop out or not; so often they are inserted fully up into the anus. Put it in too far and you have a problem because they can be hard to get out. If they make it past the guards they then meet the druggie they have been set up with on the visit.

The visitor will probably go to the toilet before they meet and retrieve the wrap. It is usually palmed in the hand and transferred in a handshake.

Others favour having a cough and so transferring it to the mouth, holding it alongside the tongue next to the gum. Some serious research needs to be done in prison about prisoners' incredible immune systems because frankly how they don't die of infection is one of the great mysteries in life.

If a large quantity of balloons are passed to the druggie, they all go 'up the chimney' or plugged, both drugs and mobile phones, until later. Then the druggie back in his cell has a wait to find out whether everything that has gone in is coming back out again or whether there have been any breakages. The inmate that organised the visit will have his people on standby to account for everything that has been passed. Once fished out of the loo (and hopefully well rinsed off) the druggie might be allowed to keep a quarter of the deal, the rest goes into the wings distribution network around the prison. Crack, cocaine, meth, and heroin find their way into inmates' hands; the drug trade in jail is an intricate web involving coordination between inmates and associates on the outside. Which is why mobile phones are so valuable.

Shane works hard now in the gym and is getting involved in the hugely lucrative world of supplying heroin around the prison. He doesn't take drugs himself, apart from steroids; he never owes money to anyone and never backs down from any confrontation. It naturally makes him noticed. Some cons with a reputation for being busy on the drugs scene outside prison make it a point to become nodding acquaintances. Not so much promises being made, but more the opening of dialogue to be pursued later if he wants. Some lads tell Shane they could 'do with a nutter like him down their way'. He can't at this point know whether he is seen as being genuinely useful or as a psycho who is expendable.

As he makes his rounds, he stops to talk to an old man serving time for murder, someone who is going to spend his life behind bars and only leave in a coffin. The man comes towards him whistling. The man stops.

'You need Jesus in your life.'

Shane cracks up and can't stop laughing.

'You're a God botherer?'

He rambles on about his Jesus and Shane's eyes glaze over. Shane has never come across anyone before who said they were a Christian and knows virtually nothing at all about any religious stuff. In his few days of attending school it had never come up and no one on his estate or circle of friends or contacts has anything to do with it at all.

'Sorry, pal, but you're a bloody nutjob.'

He goes to walk off but the man shouts out,

'I've been in prison for years and years and years, and I will never get out again, but I am free here.'

He points to his chest.

'Free.'

DIRTY

Wherever Shane is sent, it doesn't take long for him to be sent to seg because the prisons apparently have 'intelligence' about him. It always ends up being the same security information, from different people whom he has never met, who apparently keep giving the same information. He naturally suspects it of being a simple ruse by the authorities to bang him into seg whenever they want. Sometimes different tactics are employed.

Parkhurst Prison are convinced that he was a main drug supplier so he does months in segregation there. In reality, at that time, all he sold was a few bags of heroin for an extra bit of canteen.

He is also pulled up at this time by security about a letter. Stephen Whitworth, a friend of his in HMP Durham, had run up to a prison officer and slashed him from head to chin with a razor blade, giving him 46 stitches. He then wrote a letter to Shane explaining what he had done and that he was now doing a ten-year stretch. But in this letter his friend wrote, 'It's done, I've done it.'

What he meant was that he'd attacked an officer like Shane, but the prison authorities took it to mean that he had carried out what Shane told him to do. Shane became very upset at what he took to be the whole prison system being against him, and didn't know his friend had slashed an officer until they showed him the letter.

*

This time Shane is sent to the seg for organising a hit on a prison guard. 'Hit' here doesn't mean a killing, but a particularly unpleasant assault. Shane thinks it was all a set-up from the very beginning.

The 'hit' is to be a bucket of filth thrown over the guard. Each cell contributes their own personal present while squatting over the pail. They do the business, then keep sending it on to the next cell until it is full. If anyone feels able to vomit in it then that is regarded as a bonus. It is all considered a laugh. However apart from the hideous prospect of being humiliated and the subsequent emotional shock strong enough to trigger PTSD, the long-term health consequences could be very grave indeed. The range of life threatening and damaging infections contained in this mass of faecal matter and body fluids is no joke.

The guard in question has been effective at stopping drugs getting into the wing.

A young prisoner has volunteered and told the others he will do the job if he is paid. He wants ten bags of heroin, five up front, five after the hit. However, there are doubts; a hint is given that he might be a grass laying the finger on dealers in the block. Shane somehow ends up with the job of testing him out to see if he is a grass. If he gets banged up again in seg, then so be it. Shane, a lad called Michael from London, and John are told by a source they are being watched and the young volunteer is working for the guards. So the lad is given five bags and, after a good night smoking it all, is taken from his cell in the middle of the night, gives his testimony and is then sent to another prison. He had been a plant, and Shane is off to seg, but at least the other lads can get on with the business without further interruptions. Shane trusts that he will still get his cut.

After about a week in the seg again, Shane sits and thinks, 'Sack it,' it's time to fight against the system again. His constant mantra about always winning and never giving up cuts in again. He smashes out the little square glass window in the cell door and officers come to see what was going on.

Whoo hooo, it's back to war.

At first it is a variant of the previously planned hit. He gets a bottle of Radox and uses it instead of the toilet, which apparently requires a great deal of precision. It is left to fester until he deems it sufficiently potent. He presses his cell buzzer and waits. Eventually an officer comes to the door.

'I need your help.'

Shane's face looks pained as if in distress. His hand holding the bottle is out of sight as he rests it on the wall. The door opens a crack; the officer doesn't come in but looks carefully through the opening.

Shane rambles on. The guard notes his body

230

language and relaxes slightly himself; Shane doesn't look like he is going to be a danger.

He relaxes a moment too soon. Shane squirts the bottle into his face and bursts out laughing as the guard falls over backwards trying to wipe the filth from his eyes and mouth and then doubles up as he starts to gag and throw up.

They seal his door with a large Perspex sheet that will only be opened once they see Shane standing against the back wall with his hands in the air.

There is one thing Shane hasn't tried yet, but he read about it in an article about Bobby Sands, the IRA killer. A dirty protest... it sounds unpleasant but actually it is worse for the guards once you get your head round it.

A dirty protest is where everything that drops out of your backside gets smeared on to the walls of the cells, especially the handles on the doors, everywhere the guard will touch. You strip off and smear it over your body. You sleep and live in filth but, when you think of it, it's yours, it's a mess but it's your mess. For the guards it's horrible, it speaks of something so deep and fundamental in our nature about the abject: that which we all find instinctively and utterly revolting.

The guard comes into the seg and puts his hand in a sticky brown turd perched on the handle.

'Arggh, you bastard!'

The alarm goes off and the full horror of Shane's cell is apparent to everyone who comes to look in.

It's as if Jackson Pollock has been let loose with a gun filled with diarrhoea. It's on the shoes of the guard and he must have touched his uniform on the side of the doorpost as he came in, and there is Shane standing head to toe in rectal camouflage. He won't leave his cell to go to the showers, the only way he will go is if they carry him, he won't leave the cell unless they clean it.

So it's bio-suit time; it looks like they are treating him for Ebola. The trouble is you can't fight in those suits, as they find out to their cost. You must have seen crime scene cops wearing them on TV. However in the prisons the disposable, polypropylene white hazmat overalls are worn over the top of the riot gear and become surprisingly restrictive. They are worn with the hoods up over their hair and then their helmets go on top. The problem is that if they wear the face masks they can't take in enough oxygen to sustain a fight, but they really need the masks and goggles to protect themselves from all the exotic turd decorations.

Seven men are at the door of the cell, Shane is psyching himself up in his cell, dancing around stark naked, all covered in faeces.

He is shouting,

'Come on, I'll kill the lot of yers.'

He is pumped up, psyched up and ready to rock and roll.

The guards look about as likely to run as to fight.

Someone slinks away and the guards wait, no doubt

feeling like a bunch of plonkers in their suits. They are very hot, sweat starts running down their brows and getting behind their goggles, stinging their eyes, which they can't rub because they are holding a shield in one hand and a big stick in the other.

Shane is getting a bit fed up; you can only bounce around before a fight for so long before it seems a bit artificial.

He goes to the door.

'Look, lads, is this on or not?'

Someone is coming down the hall, not a guard, someone from management.

The guards part and let him through. His white suit is stretched alarmingly; it looks two sizes too small. He isn't wearing a mask, as he needs to talk, a mistake.

'Oh, good grief.'

The smell hits him and he goes green.

'Look, Shane, this has got to stop.'

Shane feels determined to keep up the pressure, so starts head butting the cell door. The officers and the manager flinch as he keeps up the beat. One guard feels his throat go dry while at the same time his pants grow alarmingly damp; he doesn't want to fight Shane. He watches the head go back and forth thumping into the door.

Shane carries out a reasonable conversation while still thumping his forehead into the metal door.

'We knew that lad was a set-up. THUMP

'We were just testing him. THUMP

'No one was getting hurt.' THUMP

The smell hits the manager again and he gasps for breath, his glasses are steaming up.

'Yes, I'm sure, I'm sure.'

He pauses and leans in with a confidential whisper. Strangely enough the whole threat of violence has disappeared.

'I'll get you out here as quick as I can and if you'll go to the showers now and come off this dirty protest.'

His voice drops to a whisper so that only Shane can hear.

'I tell you what, if you cancel this dirty protest I'll…'

*

A short while later, Shane is in a new seg cell, washed clean and wearing clothes.

He lies back on his bed and watches the telly.

A shout goes up down the hall.

'How've ya got a bloody TV on the seg?'

'You jammy…' The air turns blue as all the other inmates join in.

Solitary with a television isn't that bad. A week later he is back on the wing and everyone has heard about what happened.

LONG LARTIN

Shane is now in jail long past his normal remission date, every fight, every infraction, has eaten up his days of possible early release, but the prison cannot keep him longer than his court-given sentences. His original and added sentences have almost been served; he is just over a year away from release.

The 'Ghost Train' tour kicks in again. Prisoners like Shane can't stay too long because of the influence they exert on other inmates. It's called the Ghost Train because the moves are sudden and at night, prisoners are whisked away without notice and find themselves at the other end of the country by morning. So this tour of maximum security prisons continues. This time it is Long Lartin in Worcestershire, a maximum security prison with a hard and brutal reputation. As usual Shane is given a chance to prove himself before they lock him up in the seg.

He lies on the bed in his pad.

'I'm free in here.' A stab of the finger into his chest. The words echo around his head.

Shane blinks open his eyes; he is constantly caught by these words. Later that day there is a letter from the resident 'nutjob' himself. Shane hasn't been able to get away from what the Bible basher said about being free. For the first time in his life he had written a letter, which for Shane was a really big deal. He has asked the lifer some questions and the reply has come back fast.

He tears the envelope open and reads. It is ten pages, on both sides. It turns out to be predictable twaddle about Jesus. Shane's heart drops, there is nothing there; no help at all, just rambling stuff. He figures the guy is one step off believing he's Napoleon if he thinks all this stuff is real: 'Jesus loves you', 'He sets you free', 'He is real', 'you gotta turn to Jesus'.

He puts it to the back of his mind and life goes on. Shane becomes desperate for any distraction, and puts his name down for one of the education sessions. He is in his cell when the shout is up on the landing and the door clicks open. These prison movements are very tightly controlled, prisoners move around but only to their approved location: work, gym, education, whatever…

He arrives with a bunch of other cons outside the education block waiting for the guards to check him off the list. Inside the tutor is waiting, the module is called 'Preparing for Work Outside Prison'. Thrilling, just the same cycle of things repackaged into another course and of no relevance to where he is. He knows that when he gets out it will only be for a couple of weeks at the very most until he has his revenge. His plans are moving on, he has contacts already checking out where people live, the prison officers have been traced, those who grassed him up are back in Peterlee and he knows their addresses.

His night of revenge is still his biggest focus. He goes over it in his mind when he is alone in the dark of his cell and without fail the hairs on his arms and on his head seem to stand on end; it is electrifying. His plans are so strong he can virtually see it all unfold like a movie.

'Name?'

He's been distracted and hasn't heard the guard speak.

'Name.'

Shane is new to the prison, the guard will have heard the name in management briefings, but he hasn't seen him before.

'Shane Taylor.'

The guard looks up at Shane. Yes, he knows the name, the guard is sharper now, casualness gone. He stares at Shane.

'You're not in the book.'

Shane feels wound up inside, he hates being messed around because he knows they do it on purpose.

'What, after I've come all the way down here, what are you playing at?'

The guard sets his jaw.

'Not in the book.'

Shane is going red in the face, and the guard is now wondering whether he should be ready for trouble, his thumb moves towards the button on his radio ready to call for help.

'So what am I supposed to do now?'

The guard can't let him in, his name isn't on the list, the last thing he wants is to let Shane in only for him to go all psycho during the class and kidnap the lecturer as a hostage, or beat someone up. Neither does he want to have a fight here and now. He comes up with that time honoured idea of bureaucrats worldwide, make it someone else's problem.

'Look, there's the chapel, there's something going on, try that instead.'

Now the chaplain plays an interesting role in prisons. New prisoners are often given the tip from those who have been in the nick before.

'Get to know the chaplains – it doesn't matter if you're religious or not, they don't care. Ask to have a chat with them for pastoral reasons soon after arriving, they are good but, even more important, if you need help or a favour they are a good place to start. They are no more able to break the rules than anyone else, but they seem to exercise more common sense than others in the system.'

In bang-up they also have the benefit of being pretty accessible. If you spend all the time you are allowed to outside your cell in the corridors or on the wing, you will see them wandering around at least once a day; all the other supposed sources of help tend to involve a guard, or filling in a form. So chaplains have a type of special status among the cons.

So Shane goes into the chapel. There are a bunch of men gathered around a table with a TV perched on it. The chaplain is Eddie Baker, an older man but he seems alright. Well, he doesn't have two heads, and isn't frothing at the mouth. There is an external helper, a fresh-faced young woman who seems very keen. He sits down, but it's clear that whatever is happening has been under way for a while. A posh bloke with a voice that sounds like it is full of marbles is talking on the TV. The seats are all jammed together. People shuffle and make room for him and then, as he takes his seat, he realises his mistake, he is stuck in middle. Shane is normally quite polite when he isn't angry, and he doesn't want to embarrass himself by leaving and needing to push past the other prisoners. However, as soon as the man stops talking, Shane gets up to go, until another con grabs him by the sleeve and whispers,

'Hang on, lad, they have cake.' He grins and his eyes light up.

The young woman is scanning the list for any mistake.

'Everyone is already here and I don't seem to have you down.'

'Oh, sorry miss, could you put me on? I would love to come back again.'

She smiles and asks him his name, writing it down carefully.

She must be a mind reader.

'Would you like some cake?'

'Please, if that's okay.'

And so Shane finds himself on an Alpha course. He visits over the next two weeks and some ideas attract his attention. First he had always thought that religion was for good people. In other words you become good and then join up, being good is a prerequisite for acceptance by God. In his mind it seems natural; he reckons that the Lord above is only interested if you are squeaky clean. If you are bad, then it isn't for you. Shane has already come to believe in a type of hell, and is sure he is going there. In his head, it is maybe not too dissimilar to an infernal version of the seg unit. He has a faint idea that the demonic authorities will eventually be worn down by him if need be, so hell somehow isn't going to be that scary.

On the other hand the idea of forgiveness is both foreign and incomprehensible to Shane. He comes to Alpha for the cakes but on the third week Eddie asks him for a word in private.

'I've never invited someone back to talk before, and if you want someone else to be here we can organise that, but I feel as if I need to talk to you. Could you come back this afternoon?'

Shane isn't bothered about a chaperone, if anyone tried anything funny they weren't long for this world, but there is something about the obvious sincerity of the man that has got him interested. Eddie is short, slightly stocky, with a shock of dark hair, best described as 'getting on' in years, but he is clearly someone who cares and Shane sees that he is troubled.

Later he is seated in the dining area eating his meal, and he looks around the room. Long Lartin is a tough place and he has no friends here. In the last three weeks since his arrival he has started to make links with the lads who are handling some of the drugs on the wing. He can't quite decide whether or not to meet the chaplain or have a conversation with a man about some heroin. He takes his tray back to the slops bay and looks at his watch, he decides he might as well go and find out what Eddie wants first.

He arrives at the door of the chapel to find that Eddie is inside on his knees praying. He knocks and goes in. Eddie stops his praying and scrambles to his feet.

'My knees are shot, give me a moment.'

'Who shot them, I'll get them for you.'

Eddie's eyes widen in alarm,

'No, I mean…'

'Hey Eddie, joke, you know, just chill.'

'Oh yes, I see, very good.'

Shane patiently watches him get up and sit down on one of the two chairs facing each other; Eddie waggles his hand towards the chair.

'Sit down, please… sit.'

Shane lowers himself into the chair and it gives a little warning creak. Shane is big; he has been working out and has been on the steroids. He is like a man mountain next to Eddie. There are cups and a pot of coffee ready, Eddie pours.

'Okay Shane, I believe that God wants me to tell you something.'

'Fire away.'

Shane sits back and takes a sip of coffee.

'I'm going to say some verses out of the Bible, Shane. Is that okay?'

Shane shrugs his shoulders.

'No one is righteous. Not one. We all fall short of the glory of God.' It tells us that in the letter that Paul wrote to the church at Rome. Do you know what that means?'

Shane is holding the cup in his hand but not drinking.

'Everyone's messed up?'

'Exactly, Shane, everyone. Me, you, everyone in here.'

Shane grins. 'I can believe that.'

Eddie continues, 'But everyone else too, the normal man in the street, every vicar, the prime minister, everyone.'

Shane looks at him. 'I know that, everyone messes up.' He remembers the politicians who went to prison from the early days of Peterlee.

'Okay, that's the first thing to remember. But the next is really important.

'"The wages of sin is death." Paul wrote that too, it's in the same letter. Think about that word "sin". This is what it means.'

He counts off on his fingers. He holds up the first.

'Things we have done wrong without knowing

they were wrong.'

The second finger is held up.

'Now add to that all the good things you should have done, but didn't do.'

Eddie's third finger doesn't pop up properly, so he turns his hand around and holds the three fingers together.

'Then add all that to the things you knew were wrong but still did anyway. All of that is what we call sin. And the wages, the outcome of all that, is death.'

The sound in the room has become strange; it's totally quiet. Shane puts the cup down and it seems very loud as it hits the table. Shane stares at it for a moment.

'Do you reckon that you've made those type of mistakes, Shane?'

Shane nods and sighs.

'It's all I've ever done.'

Shane takes in a large breath. 'All I deserve is death, I am death.'

Eddie suspects that Shane has something specific in mind and, though he tries to smile, it makes him want to shiver.

'Hey, don't give up yet; it isn't the end of the story, Shane. Let me tell you two more things. "For God so loved the world that He gave his only begotten Son, so that whoever believes in Him shall not perish but have everlasting life."'

Eddie's voice is filled with concern. He goes on,

'John, a close friend and follower of Jesus wrote that. Think about it.'

Eddie is back to the finger waggling. He holds up the first.

'Number one: God loves the whole world.'

The next finger joins the first.

'Number two: God loves you, not just the world but you in it. He loves you, Shane.'

Again his third finger doesn't respond as it should and Eddie forces it into position. By now in any other context Shane would have been taking the mick out of Eddie for what looked like a dodgy Ted Rogers impression. Rogers was the 3-2-1 TV quiz show bloke who had a perma-tan and a wig. But the thought leaves as fast as it came. Shane is gripped by what he is saying.

'Number three is this. If you want real life and freedom from death you must come to believe in Him.'

Shane finds that he is grasping the arms of the chair as hard as he can. Eddie goes on.

'Not perish, that means not to die…

'Not this bit…' Eddie thumps his chest.' …the body.'

He points to his heart and then his head.

'But this bit.'

He goes on,

'And believing doesn't just mean accepting that He

exists, after all if there is a devil he must know that God exists, but that doesn't mean that the devil is a Christian, does it?'

Eddie laughs weakly. It was a serious point but delivered like a joke. He isn't good at jokes so he explains carefully:

'Believing means following, trusting in, accepting. If you want to find life you must turn your back on death. If you want to be free you must decide to follow Christ.'

Shane is staring down at his feet; he is hunched over in the chair.

'Jesus said that no one was going to take His life from Him but He was going to willingly die in our place and rise again. He died in your place, He took your death, Shane, and now he is offering you His life if you want it.'

Shane's face looks set in stone, staring at the floor. He is breathing deeply.

Eddie almost doesn't know what to say next.

'Listen, Shane, God is here and He is waiting to hear what you have to say, why don't you talk to Him?

'Jesus didn't die for the good people, Shane, He died for people like you and me, and the great news is that He rose from the dead and one day we will too. Just pray. Say what comes from your heart.'

He's gone as far as he feels he can.

Shane takes a great breath and, while Eddie waits, he starts to pray for the first time in his life.

'God...'

He turns to Eddie 'What do I pray?'

'Just from your heart. Speak, pray.'

Shane takes another great breath as if he is about to jump into a diving pool. 'Look God. If you're real, come into my life 'cos I hate who I am. I hate who I've become. And...'

He stops then repeats it over and over again.

God, if you're real, please come. I hate who I am. I hate who I've become. Come into my life.'

He stops and lifts up his eyes. There is nothing there. He feels nothing, no change at all, he still feels dead inside.Eddie looks at him; concern fills his face.

Shane holds still. Then he can start to feel something inside him shift. A surge, a feeling shoots across his stomach and settles there. He can feel like bubbles inside, then the feeling starts to rise. He is startled. 'Right. Okay. What's going on here?'

The feeling is so strange and it is coming up into his chest and then to his throat. Suddenly he bursts out crying with a huge howl. Tears are streaming down his face. He sobs and sobs and sobs uncontrollably. It is as if all the tears that he failed to cry over the years are flowing now, and there are years and years of them.

A six foot six body builder in a room inside a prison is crying his eyes out. Another sob wracks his body and he shakes and shakes. Every pain, every horror in his life is being dragged out of him. Every moment of his childhood, his teens, his 20s, is coming back to

246

him. He cries for the fact that he scares his mother, cries for the people he has stabbed, both on the outside, and in the prison, he cries for the kid he left for dead in the pond back in Elemore. A great tap has been turned on and seems determined to drain every drop. He cries for his plans to kill, he cries for ever thinking he could kill, a wife, a guard, another human being.

There have been millions of conversions where tears have been shed, but not many this loud, not many with such vast reservoirs of tears emptied on to the floor. He shudders and weeps again, as he knows wonderfully and irrevocably that God is real. He just knows. He knows this is the pivotal point at which his life has changed. He is sorry for every person he's hurt, he's damaged. He sums it up simply.

'I've been wrong, thank you, God, for forgiving me.'

The guard puts his head around the door.

'You, back to your pad.'

Shane gets to his feet and grabs Eddie in an embrace that promises to squeeze the life out of him. The guard nearly panics, it looks more like an assault upon the person than a hug. Shane turns to the guard and smiles.

'Yes, of course.'

You now have a very worried prison guard. Shane Taylor has smiled at him, and didn't argue. What's he up to?

FAILURE

The sun dawns, and as Shane opens his eyes, he instantly knows that he feels different; he is a forgiven man, he is changed. He has never slept like that before, no bad dreams, no dropping into a half sleep and no fantasies about killing. Why would he want to kill? He's been wrong, so very, very wrong.

The cell doors open and Shane steps out into his free association time. A guard is lingering on the landing trying to spot potential trouble. Shane looms out of his door and makes a beeline towards him. The guard's hand goes towards his radio in case he needs help.

Shane stops in front of him.

'Just to let you know, you won't have any more bother from me, and I'm sorry.'

He holds out his hand and the guard shakes it before it sinks in what he has done. Shane smiles at him and walks off. A second guard is now worrying about what he is up to.

Shane is on a mission to tell everyone, and I mean everyone, about his newfound faith. Years later he admits that his enthusiasm meant that people probably just thought he was mad.

He runs into a cell of a lad he knows reasonably well. Tears fill Shane's eyes as he starts his story. The con looks up, face as hard as granite.

'Listen, mate, I'm eating my dinner.' He ignores Shane, who pauses for a moment then moves to the next cell, which is full of Muslims who don't seem to embrace his good news in the way he hoped for.

The grapevine works fast, people close the doors to their cells and pretend they're not in. Others bundle him out without listening to a word he says.

Some bright spark has called him 'Dot', a nickname given to him for the rest of his time in Long Lartin. 'Dot', of course, is as per Dot Cotton, an ancient granny figure in the TV soap *EastEnders*, who between drags from her perpetual cigarettes quotes Bible verses at all and sundry. Some of the others prefer calling him God squad, or Basher as in Bible basher. He wears each name as a badge of honour.

Shane tells another prison guard that he has been wrong in the head for years. Previously it was always others who were in the wrong, never himself. He accepts everything that's happened to him, even when they have beaten him up.

'I stabbed two of your officers, of course there was gonna be a response, it's all my fault, I couldn't expect you to bring me a latte and tickle my feet.'

He walks off. As he disappears around the landing, the guard is on his radio back to the managers.

Later that day, it is pretty clear what is going on. People who wouldn't have dared to speak to him are now calling him names.

'Basher, love Jesus, do you?'

Shane just smiles. The guards and inmates now all know the story; Shane has got religion. Everyone is incredulous. The wiser lags shake their heads and say,

'He's up to summat, you'll see.'

For Eddie, he knows the real deal when he sees it. The man looks different. He smiles all the time, that's the thing that's getting to everyone. Yesterday he looked like a psycho, he had mad staring eyes; when he looked at you, you felt that he was figuring out how many pieces of blubber he could carve you up into. Now he smiles, for goodness sake, smiles! The eyes aren't mad. Someone bumped into him in the canteen and nothing happened, nothing! Shane just turned his head and smiled. As ferociously as he had thrown himself into violence and thieving, he now becomes a zealous born-again Christian. The officers were obviously incredulous.

'I can't get what he's up to and it's driving me mad.'

'He said sorry to me, sorry! I had to check it was really him.'

"Yeah, well lucky you, he had me pinned down for twenty minutes telling me just how much Jesus loves me.'

'Christ.'

'Exactly.'

*

As prisoners are due for release, there are all sorts of reviews and prison management meetings to go through but when Shane is converted the authorities really want to know if it is real, and so an extraordinary meeting is called. It is headed by the deputy governor and Shane is led into the room to find around 20 people arranged in a U shape with a solitary chair in the middle where he is told to take a seat.

Present are Eddie the chaplain, an Islamic cleric, a rabbi, probation officers, social workers and prison officers. There is a nervous tension in the air; it is odd for Shane too, apart from being in the chapel, he has never been in a room with unprotected people before.

The deputy governor starts in straight away.

'Shane, within the year you will be released, do you think you will come back to prison?'

For the next quarter of an hour they get the whole story and every one of them is taken by his passion and frankness. They have been briefed before they came in, the highlights of his file clearly outlined. He has stabbed guards, organised riots, threatened to kill staff, and beaten other prisoners to a pulp. He has sold drugs within the prison, been on a dirty protest, spent incredibly long times on segregation, been sent to CSC and is listed by the Home Office as one of the top six most dangerous prisoners. And then here he is, telling them he has been wrong all his life and that he has turned his back on his old ways and surrendered himself to Jesus, the Son of God.

He doesn't want probation or to get out early, not that it's on the cards given his crimes in prison, but even so, all, including the most cynical, can't see what he has to gain if it isn't true.

The meeting ends and people go off to make their reports.

Later Eddie comes to him.

'God is using you already, Shane.'

'How's that?'

'The rabbi and I have never really spoken before, just been on our separate paths, but now we've sat down, eaten together and shared our faith. He said he couldn't believe the passion that you had.'

*

Shortly after, Shane gets his first job inside. There are lots of jobs in prison; the authorities try to encourage you with responsibility and a little more pocket money. Shane has never been trusted before but has now been given the job of assistant to the chaplain. He is the cleaner and the orderly, doing anything that's required for the chapel and the meetings.

A week or so later he turns up in the chapel to finds a woman working there. She is putting out Bibles on the chairs. It isn't an unusual thing; the chaplain often gets approved and vetted helpers, so he doesn't think much about it.

She shakes his hand. 'Are you Shane?'

He smiles and says, 'Yes'.

'I heard you're a Christian.'

Shane tells her his story as they sit down. She listens carefully as, at some length, he brings her up to date.

'The longer I'm changed, the more it hits me 'cos the more I realise what I've done. And that's the biggest thing now I'm a Christian, suddenly realising all my life I've been wrong, and all the people who I've hurt, the people who I've damaged... is hard to face sometimes. I know I'm forgiven and I believe that. But I still find myself crying for what I've done.'

She is impassive as he talks; Shane on the other hand is now in tears again. In fact he can't talk about his conversion without crying.

'...and it's just totally changed my life. But I'm glad it happened when it did 'cos if I got out, I would have been "lifed off" straightaway back in prison. 'Cos I had plans in my head. I didn't care about getting life. I had lost hope of life. Didn't have love any more, didn't have anyone to care for any more.'

The woman settles back in the chair but is silent, letting him run on. Eventually someone comes to the door and the conversation comes to an end. They shake hands.

'Are you a volunteer?' he asks.

'No.'

'What? Not in the probation service, are you?'

'No, I'm the governor of the prison, nice meeting you.'

This time it's Shane who stands shocked as she walks away. Every governor he has met before this has been in full riot gear. Even in the hearings inside the prison, where the governor sits to adjudicate on the days deducted from remission for crimes done while in prison, the governor and deputy governor would come in to hear the case in riot gear, complete with full helmet and visor, and with heavy protection all around them.

Now this governor has come into the chapel, one to one, and listened to his story. Shane drops to his knees in the chapel praying for her and thanking God that the authorities are taking him seriously. However, it isn't the end of their testing of Shane, they really wanted to know if it was real.

The months float by, more Alphas are organised, but Shane notices that other things are happening to him, things he did automatically in the past suddenly become problems to him. He no longer wants to pop pills or smoke weed, they seem wrong. As for the idea of selling drugs around the prison, he is physically upset at the idea of what his plans had been and the things he used to do. Others have seen that Shane is not the threat he was and make their own plans to get him.

Maximum security prisons are different to cons prisons. In cons prisons you are limited in what you can buy from the canteen but in maximum security you can order in whatever food you want. You can even cook your own meals and there is a kitchen on each wing. Of course every kitchen needs equipment and, unbelievably, prisoners can hire out whatever they need, pots, pans and even nine-inch kitchen knives.

On the landing is one lad who has booked out a kitchen knife to stab Shane. The man approaches him with the blade hidden up behind his sleeve and Shane only sees the blade slashing at his face at the last minute. He manages to get his hand swinging inside the arc of the knife, and punches his assailant's arm as hard as he can on the muscle. The hand jerks as if it has had an electric shock running through it, and the man almost drops the knife. Shane grabs his wrist and swings him around into the cell. The man smashes against the wall, banging his head against the breeze-block wall. Shane grabs the knife out of his loosened hand and thumps his fist hard into his cheekbone. The man's eyes roll back into his head and he starts to slump. Shane pauses for a split second, as he almost uses the knife on him, but instead bundles the man as he starts to fall and throws him out of the cell on to the landing and then slams his door. The surge of adrenaline is still sloshing around his system, his heart is beating fast and he is pumped up but then it hits him suddenly, he didn't do what Jesus told him to do: he didn't 'turn the other cheek'. He falls to his bed shocked and holds his head in his hands.

The next day he is feeling desperate, he had responded instantly without thinking, fighting on autopilot. His heart might have changed but his instincts hadn't. How can that be? How can he not have changed? He feels as though his faith has gone. It's not that he doesn't believe, it's that he himself has proved to be a failure. Now a gulf seems to open up in front of him, it seems like God is looking across an abyss to him as he stands on the brink of falling, that God is desperately disappointed with him. Shane stands shamed and feels his face go red, now the tears in his eyes are tears of defeat.

He gets dressed and waits for the buzzer to sound on the landing and for movements to begin. He is dreading it, but knows he needs to tell Eddie what has happened and to find out if there is any hope for him.

Eddie Baker is finishing a cup of coffee when Shane shambles into the chapel and slumps down into a chair.

'I've lost it, Eddie, I've let Jesus down.'

Eddie raises an eyebrow and sips from the cup.

'Oh, really?'

'I mean it, I've blown the whole thing, man.'

'Start at the beginning.'

Slowly the story comes out, the attacker with a knife, the smashing of the back of his head against the wall, the punch to the face and throwing him out the cell.

'I didn't turn the other cheek, Eddie, I didn't even think of doing it.'

He sits glum, his face sags, it is as if someone has let out all the air from a balloon, he looks ready to fold in on himself.

Eddie leans forward towards him.

'Mind if I ask you a question?'

Shane looks up.

'Naw, you can ask me anything, I won't lie.'

'Okay, Shane, what would you have done a few months ago before you became a Christian?'

'I would have taken the knife off him, carved him up to find out who put him up to do it and jammed the knife up his...'

Eddie cuts in, 'And what did you do yesterday?'

'Defended myself and threw him out of the cell.'

Shane's eyes light up.

'I just defended myself...'

Eddie is looking almost proud of Shane.

'Jesus said turn the other cheek if someone hits you, it isn't recorded what he said about defending your life, but in my book you did the right thing.'

Eddie slaps him across the leg.

'The important thing is you didn't torture him or shove the knife where the sun doesn't shine. You left him alive and virtually unharmed.'

Shane straightens up as thinks about it. 'It's true,' he realises. Just a short while ago he would have skewered him without even thinking about it. 'Something really has changed.'

Eddie goes to finish his coffee and pulls a face.

'This one's gone cold, are you going to get a fresh brew on or not?'

IMPACT

Shane is in the exercise yard and sees a Muslim man standing by himself in the middle of the compound. Mo is nervous, sweating hard despite the cold, his eyes darting back and forth. Shane goes up to him.

'Hiya, how ya doing.'

Multiculturalism is even more of a failure inside prison than out. In the 60s pop stars dreamt of a great big melting pot and saw a possible world where everyone was of mixed heritage. It didn't really work out. People usually stay in their own communities and only a few meld into the melting pot.

In prison, the village lads cluster together away from the city lads, the North from the South, the black from the white and the Islamic lads cluster together away from the infidels. So when Shane started talking to Mo it was a shock to start with, because Mo was already in trouble and therefore deeply suspicious of everybody. Someone had suggested that he had grassed up another Muslim prisoner. That was about the worst thing that can happen in a maximum security prison. Now no one will speak to him, not in his own group or any other. Mo stands in the middle of the yard, he can't afford to go anywhere on the periphery, he must stay where he can most easily be seen. He is tooled up and waiting to be attacked. His toothbrush has been sharpened to a point after hours of working it against the breeze-block walls of his cell. It's a sharp enough shiv to shove into someone and do serious damage. He holds the head of the toothbrush in his hand, the handle up his sleeve. It isn't much but it's something. He expects that as he starts to come in from the yard someone will get close. Someone might block his path, someone else might get in the way of a guard and it will come fast. So when Shane walks up, all bright and breezy, he is terrified.

They have never talked together before but Mo realises that Shane is unlikely to be the one sent for him; it will come from within his peer group.

'You wanna keep away from me, if you know what's good for you.'

'Why's that?'

'Someone's said I'm a grass, I'm not, but that doesn't matter now.'

'Ah, I'm not worried, I've got Jesus.'

Mo is less than impressed as Shane tells his story to him.

'Tell you what, Mo, I'm going to pray that Jesus will protect you.'

'It will take more than him to get me out of this.'

'We'll see.'

Once back inside Shane is on his knees praying for Mo.

'Lord, restore him; don't let a hair on his head be harmed. Let them forget about it, let them just let it go and get him out of danger. Protect him, Lord, and reveal yourself to him.'

A week goes by, Shane calls past his cell, 'Still praying for you, Mo.'

Two days later Mo comes into Shane's pad, he is shaking.

'You've been praying for me?'

'Yeah, I told you I was, still am. Has something happened?'

Mo sits down.

'This morning they all started talking to me again, it's as if the last week hasn't happened, it's weird, it's as if they've somehow forgotten all about it. I just can't understand it.'

Shane laughs.

'That's exactly what I've been praying for, Jesus loves you, Mo, and wants to be your saviour.'

Mo gets up and as he leaves says,

'Yeah, well, thanks.'

It doesn't take long for the new realities to bed down. Now Shane is not someone to be scared of. He had only been in Long Lartin a short time before his conversion so he wasn't well known, and new prisoners who arrive just hear him called Dot and feel happy to take the mick. Every now and again, though, there is a reminder for inmates and staff. Jody is serving time for attempted murder. He was the shooter on a 'two on a bike' job. All down to drugs of course. The target had been watched carefully, they knew the car he drove about in. While he was in his house someone went up to his car and put a nail through the tyre on the front driver's side. As the car drove off, the bike followed way back in the distance. It wasn't long before the tyre went down and the driver was forced to stop. When he got out to check the tyre and was bending down, the bike was suddenly alongside and the target was a sitting duck for the gunman. Bang bang, you're dead or, well, you're supposed to be. In fact the target lived so Jody is only doing time for attempted murder. It still gives him good hard man status.

Every time he passes Shane it's effing Jesus this, and effing Jesus that. Shane just smiles and ignores it. While he is personally insulted by him, he keeps thinking in his head about how the Apostle Paul said we would be called on to suffer for our faith. However the Ghost Train has deposited someone from one of Shane's old prisons that used to know him well. Liam, a young man from Manchester, is in for two murders, he would pedal past members of other gangs and blow them away.

When Liam sees Jody get in the face of Shane and insult him he can't believe his eyes. He has a private word with Jody. When Liam has finished telling Jody about who Shane is and what he has done in other prisons, he does a rapid re-think about winding him up. They all believe Shane's got religion and means it but, there again, if he ever wakes up and decides it was just a phase, no one wants to be the first person to insult the old Shane and learn how to fly off the top floor of the wing.

The inmates divide into the 'let sleeping dogs lie brigade' and the 'let's take the mick bunch'. The betting odds run about evens and everyone waits to see how it works out.

Another time two prison officers are having a go about Jesus to Shane, swearing about Jesus as much as they can to wind him up. Shane is quoting Bible verses back to them. They are walking along one of the landings as Shane is heading back to his pad. Some of the Muslim lads join in and start swearing about Jesus too. Shane notices that Mo has joined in with their insults. He walks up to him and says quietly,

'After all you've seen, I thought you would have asked Jesus into your life by now.'

Mo's face is impassive but he whispers back so quietly that Shane has to strain to hear. Mo walks off with the rest of the lads. The words said so quietly stay with Shane.

'...How do you know I haven't?'

Shane stands and watches as they walk off.

*

One day a sudden cell inspection takes place on Shane's pad. Five or six officers arrive, Shane is made to stand on the landing while they go through everything with a fine-tooth comb, they are searching for anything, phones, drugs, weapons and it is a totally thorough search as if they expected to find something. One officer stands at the door up close to Shane, goading him inches away from his face.

'How's your f...ing Jesus treating you these days? You're a f...ing nutter, soft in the f...ing head.' He moves off into a foul-mouthed blasphemous rant about Jesus.

The other prison officer standing with Shane is a woman. She watches impassively. From inside the cell there is a shake of the head, nothing found. The guard is still ranting away but starts to look disappointed as the search comes to an unsuccessful end.

Shane looks into the face of the guard who has been insulting him.

'Do you mind if I ask you a question?'

He stops swearing.

'What?'

'Would you have spoken to me like that a few months ago when I first came here?'

The guard stops.

'So, I guess that means you know I'm changed, doesn't it? You wouldn't have dared otherwise.'

The woman standing next to him draws in a sharp breath.

The first guard marches off with the others coming out of the cell. Only the female guard is left with Shane.

'I'm impressed with how you handled that.'

She smiles and walks off. Shane is left wondering how much of all that was a pantomime, complete with the demon king, maybe as a test by the governor on how much he had changed and whether he can be goaded.

THIRTY THREE

2007

RELEASED

Maz is waiting for Shane. She thinks back to the phone call months before.

She was having a cup of tea when the phone rang. Shane called when he could and she had balanced the cuppa on the arm of the sofa as she settled herself for a chat. The calls could be long or very short depending on the queue of people lining up on the wing, but she hoped it was going to be a longer one, although she couldn't be sure.

'Mam,' he sounded excited, 'I've been to church.'

'Shut up, you idiot.' She had laughed and started to cough.

The next thing she heard on the phone was sobbing. She sat up sharply, nearly dislodging the cup from its perch.

In the middle of all the sobs she could make out the words 'I only went for the cake'.

Her brow furrowed up and then it struck her and a broad grin set in. She suddenly got it; he'd got a scam on the go. The only problem was that she couldn't see the angle. He was due for release, there were no parole hearings to take place, and he had served his full term. He wasn't coming out on licence.

'Shane, what you being stupid for? There's no such thing as Jesus.'

*

A few weeks later she is sitting in the back of a car with her sister Cath, outside Full Sutton Prison where Shane has been transferred for his final weeks. They are waiting in the car park, Cath's husband at the wheel, and they all can't help themselves from looking at the clock. He was expected out at ten but it's now quarter past. The security always takes some time to clear. You get back your clothes and any items you had when you were first nicked. Of course years have gone by, and old clothes won't fit, he has worked out in jail and is far bigger than when he went in. The mobile phone he had when he was arrested is out of date and superseded by smartphones, fashions have changed, after a long stretch there are always tensions on coming out. Some cons hate it outside and say to the guards 'see you next week' on their way out: they will have a night or two on the town, find a woman, get plastered, then purposely get arrested, all for the security of a roof over their heads, food, regular drugs and the camaraderie of the wing.

The doors open and there he is, he waves.

Even before he reaches them Cath says,

'He's never ever gonna come back to jail.'

Maz turns to look at her.

'He will, he will be back in a couple of months.'

Then suddenly he's in front of the car, they are out and it's all kisses and cuddles.

*

'I'm never ever going back here.'

Cath looks at Maz, and smirks with an all-knowing look on her face.

The days turn into weeks; he is renting a flat although often hanging out at his mother's house. Now the reality of the new Shane is sinking in. His family have moved from thinking his conversion is a scam of some sort, and are wary of getting into discussions with him, all he wants to do is tell them about Jesus.

He has gone round to people he has hurt or stolen from and asked them for forgiveness. Not an easy time for anyone.

*

Imagine.

You are sitting with your feet up watching the telly. There's a knock at the door.

A large figure looms on the doorstep, their outline visible through the window in the uPVC door. You open it and there stands Shane. You panic, why's he here? Does he know you grassed him up? Is he going to hit you first or nick your money? Instead he smiles

267

and says, 'Hiya, do you mind if I come in?'

Your heart tells you to run out of the back door fast, your head tells you it might make matters worse; he will catch you. He leans forward into your space.

You manage to mutter, 'No, come in.'

You get back into the living room, trying to remember if you have left anything valuable in view.

'Do you know why I'm here?'

You manage to shake your head.

'No, Shane.'

'Thought one of the lads might have told you I was coming round.'

Your mouth is dry, your stomach is heaving.

'I need a word, it's important.'

He turns and looks you full in the face.

'I'm sorry for everything I've done in the past and I hope you can forgive me.'

Your hand is being grasped hard. You do a double take, you look for the angle.

'Let me tell you what happened.'

Later after he has gone, you mull over what he has said. He's obviously had a breakdown or something. A while later you find yourself acknowledging that something has happened, there is something about him that is very different.

*

Shane needs to claim benefits and so finds himself in the Job Centre wading through the mire of red tape to fill in a claim. Those who have been around a while have seen him in the building. It might be ten years since he claimed but his file is thick and covered in red flags. He stands in the queue waiting to see his Job Centre advisor. Many of the other lads claiming benefit know him and there is a long line of slaps on the back or shouts of 'when did you get out?' going the rounds. It comes to his turn and he disappears behind a screen affording some attempt of privacy from the people waiting in the queue.

After a while there is the sound of a woman crying from behind the screen. Heads pop up all over the room, security guards rush over. Shane is sitting looking concerned at the woman who has broken down in a flood of tears. Before anyone can get involved, she waves away her colleagues.

'Sorry, Shane, keep going.'

She is dabbing her eyes as he shares his story with her. She sobs out, 'I want what you've got.'

She chokes back yet another sob.

'If you only knew my life right now, I need Jesus too.'

Some people laugh at him or people want to know more, but everyone has a reaction

THIRTY FOUR

2008

SAM

Shane was visiting his cousin when her friend Sam walked in. Sam is young, in her early 20s, petite, pretty, with long dark hair. Her first impression of Shane was that he was big, soft and kind. When she found out he was a Christian, and of course that didn't take long to happen, she was confused and puzzled. She had never been to a church and knew absolutely nothing about Christianity or Jesus. It was as if he was speaking a foreign language to her. She didn't know about his criminal past either 'til later. She only knew he got tongue-tied and shy when she was in the room, and she felt much the same. Sam had had a difficult background and distrusted men. She had good reason to feel as she did; she had been badly treated by men in her life, so she was surprised to find herself asking Maz for his phone number. Unbeknown to her, Shane was asking Maz if she could find out Sam's.

Given just how long Shane had been in youth and adult prisons, it wasn't at all surprising that he had never really been in a relationship before.

In his early teens the only time he had the chance for sex while locked up in a children's home was in a joint institution where there was a girls' wing and a boys' wing with barbed wire crammed heavily between the two. Night-times were all on lock down so all the furtive and covert liaisons took place during day-time mixed school lessons, where girls and boys would separately excuse themselves to go to the toilet, meet up and explore the more practical side of the biology curriculum. There were short times in his mid and later teens that he wasn't locked up, usually it was casual and not more than one night stands.

There was one longer relationship of nearly two years but it was difficult and doomed to fail.

So it isn't surprising that Shane felt bowled over when he met Sam; he had never been in love before. Shane had joined a church when he left prison, and he naturally invited Sam along, but she wasn't interested at all. They fell in love very quickly and Shane and Sam were in a full relationship virtually straight away. It was a tough time, the temptations of prison had been managed well; he could stand up to threats of violence and abuse but, outside, the threats to his faith were of a softer and more alluring kind.

Sam did eventually go along with him to church, but it didn't seem to make sense to her. She listened to Shane, smiled when he talked about Jesus, and then got on with her life. Shane had been in touch with a former paramilitary member from Northern Ireland who like himself had got converted in prison. Based in Manchester, David Hamilton was now a pastor of a Pentecostal church and Sam was persuaded to come along to hear his story.

David Hamilton had spent more than a decade

in jail after becoming a member of a Protestant paramilitary group. His conversion had meant that he had to re-evaluate his life and come to understand just how wrong he too had been. He talked candidly about his past, about how he became locked in a cycle of paramilitary violence; about living in an environment that was filled with hate; and about his life being under threat even as he tried to move on from his troubled past.

He preached from the pulpit with a compelling voice in a strong Irish accent.

'I grew up in Belfast and was only a teenager when the troubles began. Bobby Sands and I played football together as boys. I could have easily been an IRA man, it just depended which side of the street you were on, but really as a result of being beat up by a group of Catholics, simply, they told me, because I was Protestant, I began to fight against them.

'Both sides found it was safer to be involved in a gang. One night a man came into our youth club and asked for volunteers to join the UDA, and most of the gang members joined overnight. That's what started my involvement in the paramilitaries.'

Hamilton served 12 years in jail for the part he played in bombing a factory, as well as taking part in armed robberies. He had been given an extra year during his time inside for bad behaviour. Prison wasn't easy, not least because it offered little protection from the violence raging on the outside.

'It was hard at that time because you were suddenly put in jail with men who were your enemies outside.

There were men actually murdered, and there were men blown up in jail.'

But something happened while he was in prison that changed his mindset. He came to believe that God had spared his life.

'I'd been shot a couple of times. I'd been blown up. I always just thought I was lucky to survive. But that night I believed it was divine intervention, not luck.'

He had rubbed shoulders with some of the most notorious characters from the troubles. Bobby Sands, his childhood friend, became the IRA hunger striker that tried to rally a very hard-line nationalist position. The comradeship of their early years turned to a fierce hatred as the religious divide became too much for the former friends to bear.

He recalled an attempt being made on his life as he spoke in church after his release.

Republican paramilitaries shot three men dead at the door, as well as another eight people inside. Mr Hamilton's pregnant wife lost her baby through the stress of living through the troubles. The couple had to move to England because of on-going threats.

David finished his preaching by bringing his story up to date and how he is amazed that he is now able to return to his homeland, and even share the message of peace with those who were on the other side of the divide.

'I was in the Falls Road, which is the main republican area in Belfast, and I actually sold some of my books there last year. It's amazing that someone who was involved in the UVF could actually go up the Falls Road and speak to a church of 200 Roman Catholics, and be received and even welcomed. That shows there is a change in attitude. The IRA blew up four members of my family in the Omagh bombing. Of course, people were angry. That turns into bitterness and they can get a hard heart. But what I have found is that the hatred and animosity I had did more harm to me than the people I was hating.'

He went on to tell the story of meeting people who have tried to kill him, including the man who shot him three times.

'You re-live it all when you suddenly come face to face with the person who did the injury to you. Forgiveness is a message people need to hear for their own sake. But not only have I learned to forgive but I've met people who are willing to forgive me for my past. It works both ways.'

For Sam it is a bolt out of the blue, she had been abused in her childhood and the message of forgiveness is a powerful one that reaches out to her. Shane is bent over and has his head in his hands constantly praying for Sam.

'God please save her…'

He is so intense in his prayers he doesn't see her get up out of her seat.

Sam walks down to the front of the church, joining scores of others who are responding to the call to come forward and accept Christ.

Eventually Shane sees her return, but thinks she

274

had nipped out to use the loo. When Sam tells him she has made a decision to follow Jesus he dances with joy: he literally dances, the big lump with two left feet actually dances a jig.

It is interesting to record the way that their story worked out. They moved in together but were later surprised when the church leaders pointed out that for Christians the Bible teaching is clear that sex is only appropriate for those within marriage. They checked out the Bible themselves and realised it was true. It hadn't dawned on them before. They had thought once you were shacked up together it was all alright. Nobody their age seemed to get married. They moved out to separate houses, pledged to wait 'til after the ceremony and planned a very quick marriage. They made a solemn and heartfelt pledge to each other, that Christ was going to be the most important thing in their lives together.

If Jesus wants his followers to keep sex within marriage, then that's what they will do. They aren't just believers, they are followers.

THIRTY FIVE
2008

PAUL

For Paul Venis being locked up in prison shouldn't have been a total surprise: he had been in trouble all his life, his parents were involved in the drug trade, and he had led a very violent life. He lies on his bunk with a great heavy lump in his throat.

He loves his wife and kids more than anything, but violence has literally come knocking on his door. The images of what happened are constantly in his mind's eye. The man at the door with a gun, his own retaliation, standing up in court and hearing the 'guilty' verdict, and then the awful moment the judge is passing sentence. Then it all becomes a whirlwind, being taken down from the dock, not being able to see anyone, being whisked away and banged up. Since his early run-ins with Shane he has become known as a fearsome fighter. He took part in bare-knuckle fights and underground prize fights all around the UK, so when prison looms he expects it to be a walk in the park, but it isn't.

Life in prison just isn't how he expects it to be. When the doors of the cell lock on that first night Paul lies on his bunk bed and feels the walls moving in closer and closer. He discovers he is claustrophobic. He finds that he rails against the injustice of it. He is too good to be in jail, what was he supposed to do when people came to his house and threatened him and his family? He had to respond.

'What else could I do?' It echoes around his mind, 'What else could I do?'

Everything Paul knows about prison is from the movies; all the clichés and tropes. He expects to be challenged by a big guy that runs the wing, he expects to beat him up and become the kingpin that rules the roost. But it isn't like that at all. He decides that for him it is like being in a youth club for grown-ups. For him that's what it's like. What frightens him about it all is just how easy it is. Three meals a day, roof over your head, Telly…' it's mental… mental.' Days merge, time slips by and you can forget who you are and what is really important.

Paul is an angry person and it doesn't take much to rub him up the wrong way. The route to surviving prison he decides is to trust absolutely no one. It is surprising how unchallenging it is for him to be in here, until the door locks. The walls then get closer and he looks at the pictures BluTacked to the wall. One is of his wife and two beautiful kids. They're both in school, and he wonders what the other kids are saying to them about their dad. That breaks him and he hides his tears.

Whether or not the lad in the pad next door is listening to Paul trying to hold back his sobs at night is impossible to know. He is either deaf, or a wise lad to pretend that he doesn't hear a thing. The other picture on the wall is of Paul and his dogs.

Two weeks into his sentence, Paul gets up in the middle of the night and carefully takes the pictures down, rolls the remaining BluTack off the wall and sticks them all away. The photos are hidden in a book and kept away from sight. The walls still move in tight, but his crying has stopped. He understands that he can't do his time while holding on to his world outside.

Talking about it now and looking back he says,

'You know it changed me. It drove me crazy. But I coped and got on with it. I'd be lying if I said I didn't meet some decent lads in there. You know, lads who I thought were similar to me, wrong time, wrong place, simple, you know? You pay the consequences, you get on with it. I'd never ever wanna go back to prison, I tell you that.

'I hadn't seen Shane for years; we'd gone our separate ways. I'd been in prison a while and my auntie sent me a book she thought would help. She was a Christian and it was about people who were involved in criminality and had their lives changed by God. I remember opening this book and seeing Shane's face on a photo inside the book and he stood there, big smile on his face. The mad psychotic look had gone. Even in this book I could see that. I read it and I was like, wow, that's a bit mad. And I rang my auntie and I told her I was reading the book.'

I said, 'I know this guy.'

She went, 'Oh, you know him, dear?'

I went, 'Yeah.'

She went, 'That's funny because he wants to come and visit you.'

'I hadn't seen Shane for about ten years so I wondered if he would really remember me. When he came in, as soon as he walked in the doors, I could see he was different. He'd changed from having a psychotic, murderous face to a kind face, you know? Like a humble face. He looked like a humble person. I was absolutely amazed.'

'He came over and gave me a big hug and said, "I'm Shane."

'I said, "I remember you." And funnily enough he remembered all the run-ins that we've had as well.

'I came to believe that it was God that let us meet when we did. We hadn't seen each other for a long time and then all of a sudden he comes with this message of forgiveness and love. I was pleased he didn't overpower me with the God stuff. He just answered the questions that I got to ask. We'd built a friendship any way over the years and I do believe only God can change a man like that, you know. His story is unbelievable and it affected my life. It will affect my life forever. His story, the way he is now, it's made me become open minded about God.

'When I got released from prison, my mindset was different; I was determined to come out of crime and never go back to prison. There was a gym in Southbank and I thought, "I'll go in, just to try to do something positive, to take my mind off things." I walked into this gym and it turned out to be a boxing gym. I'd never been in there before but the man who was running it let me use it for free because he knew I was just out of prison. He just wanted to help me stay on the straight and narrow. I was doing a bit of boxing, bit of kickboxing, just to keep myself fit. I'd only been going a couple of days when I was told that a world champion in kickboxing was coming down to spar with one of the heavyweights in the gym. He only got two rounds out of him and the heavyweight was all done in. The owner was in a bit of a fix, he came over and said, "You can fight can't you, Paul?"

'I went, "Yeah, yeah, I can fight."

'"Do you wanna do a round with him?"

'"Yeah, well.. I, I'll do a couple."

'After six rounds with him I had dropped him twice with body shots, absolutely battered him and this kid was the world champion, you know what I mean?

'So when I'm finished with him they're all like, "Oh, please, will you go and fight for us, you've got to."

'I said, "Right, I'll turn professional. I'll fight for yous but I wanna turn pro." I was thinking about money to provide for the family. I felt right.

"I'll turn pro, set a couple fights up for me."

'The trouble was I was waiting for contracts with people who didn't want to fight me, so I moved to the mixed martial arts and started learning how to do the right kicks and elbows and knees, and I took to it, absolutely loved it. I was quite a disciplined person now. I was also spending time, a lot of time, with Shane and getting more and more open minded about Christianity, which was beginning to change me. It was helping me being dedicated to this sport, and I started doing it for a living.

'I was fighting for titles, I had a big fight, a British title, fought a lad who no one wanted to fight. I stopped him in the second round; it put me on the map straight away. All the money went up, and I started to earn a decent living, you know. Eventually it led me to fighting for the European title, where I stopped the lad, again in the second round. And then I had my big fight just before Christmas, fought for the world title, and stopped the lad in the first round. I became the British, European, and World K1 Heavyweight Champion, which is something that I wanted to accomplish, you know I'm very proud of what I've been able to do.'

Paul won every one of his fights by knockout and has one of the most lethal punches in the world. However something happened that meant him giving up fighting.

He went on telling his story:

'I've always had my struggles. I've always battled in my head, with ego, stuff like that. Fighting in the ring was always about channelling rage into controlled violence.'

His determination to stay away from crime meant he found the perfect outlet for his deep-seated anger; it kept him legal and legitimate but didn't deal with the inner turmoil. However his spiritual journey was coming to a head. He found himself suddenly coming to faith. It wasn't as sudden as Shane's headlong rush into God's love but was just as pivotal. Shane invited him to go along to a connect group in Newcastle. He was still unsure about God, but on that night had an experience where he surrendered his life to God and was suddenly filled with the Holy Spirit.

Paul says, 'I had that experience and it's something I can't deny, you know. And God revealed himself to me and I've been baptised, I'm born again and I'm a Christian.'

The impact was immediate. Paul suddenly realised he didn't want to hit people for a living. It was an accumulation of things that came together. Paul wasn't daft, he knew that every time he went in the ring it made more money for others than it did for him, yet he was the one in the end that would find his health damaged and deteriorating because of the pressure of training and fighting. So at the top of his game, undefeated, unwilling to take more risk to himself and also the risk he posed to others, he gave up his fighting career. He now helps people recovering from addiction, an utterly changed man from the person he was in the prison cell.

His record is compelling. He won every single match, he defeated every single opponent, and he won every fight by a knockout in the early rounds and was never forced to go the distance. And here it becomes impressive; he ultimately gave it up because he couldn't bear hurting anyone after his conversion.

THIRTY SIX
2018

NOW

They say that time reveals the truth of things. Whatever your favourite expression or aphorism you use about the nature of time, it is true that the biggest test anything can face is time.

More than ten years have now passed. Shane's conversion has stood that test of time. Cynical friends and relatives now, without exception, all accept that Shane is sincere. Strangely the only people who cast aspersions on his motives were small numbers of churchgoers sitting in the pews who were suspicious about him telling his story, and wondered if he was in it for fame or fortune.

To deal with the money side first, in the ten years he has worked for various Christian charities, Shane has refused to be paid more than the national minimal wage despite his growing family, and any windfall he gets goes into supporting his own charitable work of helping prisoners get on their feet when they leave prison and put their life of crime behind them. For those who are critical about how much press Shane gets, they must understand that he feels utterly compelled to share his story so that others can come to know his Lord and Saviour.

He started working with ex-cons, and then Alpha

asked him to work for them organising Alpha sessions in prison. He has stood on the stage in the Royal Albert Hall sharing his story with 6,000 people, he has been in newspapers, television interviews, GQ magazine and now a film is being made of his story.

He has five beautiful children, and considers himself blessed and extremely happy. The family all go to New Life Church Teesside in Billingham. Sam and Shane live in an ex-council house that he rents from a serving policeman.

Chris, the police officer, has 17 years of service, and works on the armed response unit. He met Shane five years ago through a family friend. They got on when they met and Shane was up front and told him he'd been inside. When Chris heard that he had been a dangerous inmate he wasn't fazed, a lot of other people he'd met have had a reputation as hard lads. He took it all with a pinch of salt and didn't really give it any credibility until it was mentioned that Shane was on the Home Office's list of the top most dangerous prisoners in the country. Chris isn't a Christian himself and doesn't hold with those beliefs but he became intrigued by Shane's story. Slowly they became good friends. When he was interviewed for the upcoming, film Chris said:

'I form opinions of people, I try not to judge but it's natural to do that, my impression of Shane is that he is a decent human being. I didn't see that other side of how he used to be. I find Shane trustworthy, I believe his story is credible, in fact I'm certain it is, I don't think it's just bravado or an act, I see Shane on a regular basis and I'm confident that he's changed.

'I find Shane's conversion miraculous, but it's not something I believe in, so it is difficult to get my head round it all, but his conversion is there for all to see. He is a different person, there's no doubt about that.

'I've certainly not seen anyone change to that degree. I think when most people come out of prison there's a lot of promises to change and I think most of it's genuine; I think most people do want to change but go back to their old life, they go back to old friends, to the same area they lived in. It's very difficult for people to start a new life. I've never seen anyone do what Shane's done, to that degree. He's completely changed. His answer is that he's done it through faith in the Lord. I find that a strange concept but I suppose there must be some truth to it because he's living proof that's it worked for him.

'I knew he was struggling living where he was living, and I was looking to buy another house, it's not a big business it's not a money earner, just a pension for the future. I'm his landlord now, I certainly wouldn't normally dream of renting a house to a serious ex-offender other than Shane, but I trust him, he's one of my best friends.'

*

If there is one man who watched Shane from an early age through to his time in prison and beyond it is Andy Smith, his youth worker / teacher at Elemore Hall and later prison officer at Holme House. He saw Shane nearly kill the boy at Elemore and then stab two of his colleagues in prison.

In an interview Andy Smith says:

'I heard what happened to my colleagues, and I was shocked, you don't want to see someone you work alongside being hurt, do you? But surprised? No. He was a dangerous individual, there's no doubt about it. I wasn't on duty that night, I obviously heard about it afterwards. Shane was evil. There's no nice way of putting it, he was very aggressive, angry, especially against authority. He used to think about ways he was going to kill prison guards and police officers. That's how bad he was.

'However when I heard that Shane became a Christian, I wasn't cynical about it because I'm a Christian too. So I believe God can change anybody's life, even Shane Taylor's. I heard through the grapevine that he'd become a Christian, but I kept my distance. I didn't get in contact with him for two, three years after his release. If he was visiting a church or group of people I would avoid it. Then I got to the point where I thought, "No, it's right to actually go and see him." So I asked the governor at the time to grant permission for me to go and see Shane, which he did. It was surreal to see the difference, if I'm being completely honest with you. Absolutely surreal.

'His aggression had gone. The anger had gone and this big softie was in front of me. It was just nice to see a totally different Shane Taylor. This guy you knew from old you'd never turn your back on. And suddenly it's like this guy is like a role model for people to follow. That's what it's all about. For all young people who think that they know it all, which Shane did, ever since I've known him, he thought he knew every single answer. He wouldn't listen to anybody. He knew best.

'For the ones who are sitting in the cells now and read his book or watch his film this is a lesson for them; if he can change, you can change. Anybody can change. I know there are bad apples in every organisation but it's important to know that in jail, prison officers will help you. They want you to reform, that's what's happening within the prisons, so people will get jobs when they get out, have somewhere decent to live, to live law-abiding lives outside. We don't want people to come back; the prison staff in general do a good job.

'Shane was given permission to come back into Holme House and actually met one of the prison guards that he'd stabbed. It was incredible to watch him come in and shake hands with John. They spent about an hour and a half talking with each other and Shane's apologised three, four, five times to the point where, when they finished the meeting, my colleague actually shook his hand and said, "Anything you need in the future, let me... by all means, ask and I'll help you."

'We are the forgotten service sometimes but actually we try to do a lot of good work with prisoners on a day-to-day basis, every single day. We don't want people to come back. As simple as that. From the governor down, we want to reduce re-offending, with the limited resources we've got, the staff in here, prison officers in here, do a brilliant job. They really do an excellent job.

'Shane is allowed to come in the prison now by the governor. I had the privilege of going with Shane to the Royal Albert Hall in London where we sat side by side, shoulder to shoulder, from both sides of the bars which was a brilliant testimony and powerful witness to everyone.'

*

Shane felt the need to go back to his old home ground and to apologise to the community for all the crimes he had committed there.

He organised a meeting in the back room of a pub and put together leaflets, which he personally handed out on all the streets where he had burgled and threatened the people.

He said:

'I'm going back to Peterlee. I want to say sorry to people. First of all I want to tell them about God and show them that there's a change in my life. But I want to say, "Look, I'm sorry. I'm sorry for what I've done. If there's anyone I've committed crimes against, I'm sorry." And if they don't forgive me, they're well within their rights. And I respect that and I understand that. But if they do, thanks, because I don't deserve it.'

Around 200 locals turned up to hear him tell his story. All his old mates, well, those who were currently out of jail, came to hear him. Others came too, people he had stolen from. They listened in a hushed silence and at the end of the meeting scores of people came forward to pray.

*

Today a slightly more mellow Maz is usually to be found at Shane's house helping with her grandkids.

'You should see Shane with the bairns, he's really good. Gets up and plays with them, loves them to bits. He tries to make up for what he missed out on when he was a kid.'

All of Sam's and Shane's kids are live wires. By nature they are all as mischievous as Shane was, but he is determined to bring them up well. He says, 'If I had kids before my conversion, they'd have had a bad upbringing; I'd have twisted their minds. Now they get to know how to live, they go to church. So God's not just changed me but he's changed the whole cycle of my family. A lot of my family were involved in something dodgy or they've been to jail. You know there's something not right there. So God for the first time cut the chain. My kids are going to get brought up in a totally different way. And so, hopefully, that has an effect on the next generation of my family, not just me.'

Shane's days are taken up with helping people, his family, and travelling around speaking at churches.

THIRTY SEVEN

ALPHA

Alpha started at Holy Trinity Brompton (HTB) in London in 1977, originally as a course about Christianity for new churchgoers and was aimed at those who had never been across the threshold of a church before. Holy Trinity Brompton is friendly but, no matter how it tries to tell itself otherwise, it is posh, and at the heart of poshland: it's just down the road from Harrods. Thirteen years after it started, Nicky Gumbel, a Cambridge man, arrived to take over as vicar. Nicky's father was an immigrant fleeing the Nazis who came to London, he was a barrister who married a barrister, Nicky's sister is a barrister and yes, you've got it, Nicky was a barrister before he entered the Church.

He wanted a way of creating discussions with agnostics in a sort of neutral space, somewhere there could be a structured discussion, but open to all who come in regardless of their views. He re-shaped Alpha, giving it a sharper focus and made it easier to understand for the man in the street. It starts up with the introductory talk called 'Is there more to life than this?' It handles the idea of what faith is and how we can examine Christianity's historic roots. He manages to make sure it never feels like church and uses food, sharing a meal together, to help people feel relaxed and to join in. The marketing is tightly targeted at non-Christians and it is very different to the rather staid Church of England norm. It has also spread like wildfire. Thousands and thousands have come to faith in Christ, millions upon millions have taken the course. Alpha operates in 169 countries in more than 66,000 locations. In an era of those who are increasingly pilloried for their faith, the average attendees are remarkably young – HTB's average age is 27. A host of stars and celebrities have been on the course.

Back in 1994, a prison chaplain in Exeter was excited to try it out with the local inmates, including Michael Emmett who was once an international drug smuggler, his father Brian and himself were in the same prison together.

Brian was old school with a reputation; he used to know the Krays. Emmett had got in with the chaplain in order to get better access to the phone, so he could call his girlfriend Daniela more often. On the outside she, it turns out, was already going along to an Alpha course along with her mate, the page three model Sam Fox. Daniela was really enthusiastic about Alpha and told Michael. When the chaplain mentioned the course, Michael spoke up about it and the governor agreed to give it a go.

Since Emmett went along, it had a kudos and others joined too. Nicky from HTB sent a team down to run it and it had an incredible response. Both Michael Emmett and Brian his dad found themselves on their knees and crying while something profound happened inside them. It wasn't just an emotional night; it utterly changed their lives. When hard men like this change, people sit up and take notice.

The government's prison dispersal policy itself became part of the way that Alpha was propagated from prison to prison. It spread like a virus, if that doesn't sound pejorative. Cat 'A's move around the nine maximum security prisons. One group of Alpha converts might find themselves spread out to all the different prisons; they in turn would lobby the chaplain to start up an Alpha. More lives would get changed and then they would be spread around again, until very quickly Alpha was established in many prisons. Michael Emmett was transferred to three further prisons, Swaleside, Maidstone and Blantyre, and he brought Alpha to all of them. His reputation meant that others came along to see what it was about. For the prison governors it was a bolt from the blue. Prison and religion had always had a strange relationship. Fake conversions were often embraced to help with parole boards, and were commonplace, but the types of conversions that were happening here were unprecedented. People were changing, really changing. When Michael Emmett was released he didn't go back to a life of crime, instead he remained committed to the faith he had found in jail, and volunteered to take it to other prisons around the world: in Hong Kong, South Africa, and South Korea.

By 2015, an amazing 250,000 inmates worldwide had completed Alpha. In Britain, it is offered in more than 80% of prisons. Paul Cowley another ex-offender who came to faith through Alpha and works with HTB, helped form a sister charity to Alpha, Caring

For Ex-Offenders (CFEO), which meets ex-cons at the prison gate, and tries to get them linked to a local church.

Figures from 2015 produce very impressive results: Alpha converts have a re-offending rate of just 17%, compared to the national average of 58% for those serving less than 12 months. Something significant is impacting on the lives of hardened criminals and that is important when you consider just what it really means. How many lives have been saved? It is not just the likes of Shane and Michael Emmett that have been 'saved' in a theological sense. It is how many other lives, their potential victims, have been saved from being murdered, how many lives would have been injured or maimed, how many houses would have been broken into, how many kilos of drugs imported, how much money would have been lost from theft and criminal damage? That is what has also been saved by their 'salvation'.

*

In the spring of 2018 Shane was invited to do a TEDx talk in Luzira Maximum Security Prison, Kampala, Uganda, with Emmy Wilson who then took him on safari afterwards. Emmy started her working life as a nurse, the last three years of which were spent nursing those affected by HIV and AIDS. She then joined the staff of Holy Trinity Brompton, London, in 1985 to begin the work of 'The Earl's Court Project' (a Christian ministry responding to AIDS, prostitution, drug addiction, alcoholism and homelessness). Emmy became involved in prison work in 1991, helping as a part-time volunteer in the chaplaincy team at HMP Holloway, the largest women's prison in London.

In December 1994 she began taking teams to other prisons in the UK to support chaplains who wanted to start using the Alpha course. Emmy has visited prisons and spoken about her work at Alpha conferences and Alpha Prison Trainings all around the world. She was the person that first took Shane back into the prisons to talk to the inmates and tell them his story.

In Kampala he went in to the jail to talk to the inmates, where of the 4,000 in the prison many were being held on death row. Unlike his own pre-prison life, many prisoners had done nothing wrong. Many had been denounced as being criminals because they refused to deal with big business that wanted land or something important from them. A simple accusation can lead to prison for years without trial and when trials happen there is often no real legal representation.

The prison is a dumping ground and a place of no hope. They all spoke English and understood most of what he said even if some of the slang and his North-East accent went over their heads.

Shane had never been abroad before, not counting prison on the Isle of Wight. In fairness to Shane, he didn't know what to expect, and by the way, he was probably the only man on safari still dressed for the streets of Middlesbrough. The lions and the elephants peered at him, not the other way around, he is a rare creature.

Shane may have been a man out of his comfort zone but the message he had was as powerful as any that anyone else could have preached. He couldn't help but remember the prisoner on life that he met in jail. The man that said, 'I'll never get out of prison but I'm free in here' as he pointed to his heart. Shane couldn't do anything about the injustice of those who were stuck behind bars through no fault of their own but his message of hope had a tremendous impact and response.

THIRTY EIGHT

EPILOGUE

When Shane's sentence was up, he had to be released. Fact. There was no legal way to keep him in prison. It is worth thinking about what would have happened if he hadn't had his 'encounter' with God and his conversion experience. Just how effective would the probation service have been? How effective would the legal system have been at stopping him killing? I doubt that many would think that there would have been many positive outcomes for Shane and for those that crossed his path.

If he had not changed, he would have been very likely to kill.

Would he have slaughtered the prison guards in their homes? Probably not, but there again... who knows. It could all have depended on the state of his mind at the time. He was clearly mentally ill, with strong sociopathic tendencies.

Would those he blamed for 'grassing him up' have died? It takes a brave person to say no. Everyone who knew Shane knew just what he was capable of. How many burglaries would he have committed? How many people would he have beaten, how many stabbed or injured, just how much money would the state have had to spend to lock him back up again? It is also a sobering thought to remember just how many 'Shanes' there are behind bars, and also free on our streets.

Alpha has its detractors, Christianity is attacked by the new atheist lobby, evangelism attacked by every politically correct group, they say it is sexist, it is racist, it is bigoted, they say it is out-dated, and it is unnecessary. On the other hand, many thank God that He still changes lives.

For those who do pillory Christianity, it is worth remembering what was written nearly 2,000 years ago in the Bible: 'There is neither Jew nor Gentile, neither slave nor free, nor is there male and female, for you are all one in Christ Jesus.'

No other creed or society in the world at that time (nor for millennia to come) was declaring an equality between religious background, race and gender. The first preachers of non-discrimination were the first Christians. The foundations of the respect movement owe a great deal to this expression of equality.

Let me paraphrase, or make a point for today, if I dare:

There is no difference between the posh and the common, the upper class and under class, the criminal or law-abiding, men, women, racial group or colour of skin, sexual orientation or how we identify: we all need to become one through accepting Jesus to be our Saviour and Lord.

And that is just what is happening with Alpha and the evangelical Christian message today. All can become one. Shane, an ex-criminal, can stand on the stage at the Royal Albert Hall with a serving prison officer and an ex-barrister, a heavyweight champion of the world, a vicar and an ex-gang member of the Krays.

Show me another cultural sphere where we can see this unity, where such a diverse group would be willing to trust the others with their lives.

Shane, Michael, Brian, Paul and thousands and thousands of others say they have been saved by Christ through Alpha courses. Hearing the good news of the Gospel message has changed millions of lives around the world. Those who might have become the victims of those converts should maybe acknowledge the bravery of those tirelessly working to bring good news into prisons and to lives everywhere.

*

The message of the Gospel and the power it has to change lives is real; it's not an emotional release that somehow cathartically discharges bad things within.

It is truth that illuminates the darkness inside all of us.

Maybe the language people hear at church is difficult to understand. If Shane was to say that God has forgiven him his sins because of what Jesus did at the cross, what would that really mean? How can we set out without jargon exactly what it means? What is sin?

Sin is about realising that you have failed to be the

person your conscience tells you that you should be.

If you have not done the good you should have done, if you have inadvertently done the things you later know were wrong, and on occasions have deliberately done things your heart was telling you not to, then you are a sinner.

This failure is what God calls sin and, don't be surprised, we are all in the same boat, it's part of the human condition. If that name 'sin' sounds old fashioned then call it failure. The fact doesn't change, we all have failed. For some like Shane, their failure is very obvious, for others who might appear on the surface to be wonderful and kind people, it lurks underneath, but it is there, we all feel guilt for bad decisions and secret desires that shame us.

*

Once we understand that we have these failures inside us, we need to decide what we have to do about it.

The easiest is that we may decide to ignore it, after all it is the human condition, it just is. We may even go so far as to refute the very notion of moral value and reject the idea of defining failure, but we cannot change if we do not accept we have a problem.

Many feel a deep underlying guilt at every one of their failures, especially those that have hurt others. When we hurt those we love, when we damage others by our actions, it becomes difficult. Do we just become hard and move on with our lives? This is the very process that drove Shane into a killer mentality and mental illness. On the other hand, if we understand that something needs to be done about our inner problem, then we are faced with what that might be.

The Christian good news is this, although sin has spoiled our spiritual nature (in fact it kills it), God has unilaterally taken action to restore us back to himself.

People often find themselves shocked by some of the basic beliefs of the Christian faith. The Bible tells us that Jesus, God the Father and the Holy Spirit are all one in nature and essence, and yet distinct in character. Jesus said, 'If you have seen me you have seen the Father.' He said, 'No man has ever seen the Father,' and that to worship Him it must be in 'Spirit and in Truth'. It is hard to talk about eternal things in our limited language and with our constrained human understanding.

Many academic thinkers have concluded that no matter how brilliant we are, we cannot explore God, although vast numbers have tried of course. Philosophy has spent thousands of years of trying to do just that. We don't need to invent religion, make up little (or big) superstitions or imaginary metaphors. To really understand, we need God to intervene and speak to us.

If we turn to the words of Jesus, He claims He is from the Father and is in unity with the Father. He is the creator of all the material universe.

300

Now plenty of others have noted that such claims are so huge, so preposterous that either they are true or Jesus was barking mad. So check out the words of Jesus yourself, try reading John's Gospel or Matthew's, or Mark's or Luke's, they are all eyewitness accounts of His life by people who were with Him.

Listen to His words, listen to Him talk about love and life. They aren't the words of someone who was deranged.

If Jesus is right, then there is a way to find forgiveness for all of our failure, or sin. Everyone knows that Christians believe that Jesus was crucified and then rose from the dead. Jesus said, before it happened, that no one was taking His life from Him but He was going to lay it down and take it back up again. He said He was going to willingly die for our sakes, and then take that life back up again. He died to pay the price of all our sins, the record of our failures, but death could not hold Him and the Father raised Him from the dead.

To deal with sin, we need to turn our back on it, to ask Jesus for forgiveness and to live in Him and for Him. Sin has a huge impact on our lives, it separates us from God. He is perfect, and our wilful and fallen nature kills off the spiritual life that we were meant to share, it also damages us mentally, emotionally and spiritually.

God is love, and loves each and every one of us. He hates what sin does to us, which is why He himself became the remedy for it.

Sin eats us up with guilt and, to accommodate it,

we either suffer or become hard. Our separation from God leaves us alone and without meaning. It is when we are restored to God that life falls into place. First, the weight of sin lifts and we feel free, then the love of God fills us and we understand that we are loved, personally and individually. Imagine that, we with all our frailties, complexities and flaws; we are loved.

A lot of people get the impression that Christians have to live by a set of out-dated rules and regulations. However it isn't like that, first we want to live to please God, we trust Him, we believe that what He tells us is for our benefit. But the other strange thing is that something changes inside us. Some find themselves freed from drugs or drink they have been addicted to for years. Yes it's true that others find that the change isn't instant, but freedom comes from within, not by rules and regulations. This is because when we come to new life in Him, He promises to give us His Holy Spirit as a sort of down payment of the heaven to come. This new life, and I hesitate to use the words 'born-again' because it has become tainted as a political term these days, this new life means that we are born again of the Spirit of God. New, changed and, inside us, we are already part of heaven.

So how to progress? Try for yourself. Pray.

Ask God to reveal Himself to you but there is one catch.

Don't pray it unless you really mean it.

Pray it if you are sincere, even if you don't yet believe. But when God starts to move in your life, whether it is moments after you pray, or some time later, embrace it, trust in Him, seek Him and let Him in your life.

What to pray? It is simple. First accept that you are a failure, you have sinned, you have done things wrong and failed to do things you should. Now be prepared to turn your life around and let go of the old ways of thinking and acting. Next accept that Jesus died for you and invite Him into your life, as Lord and as Saviour. Believe in Him and surrender your future to His plans for your life. Don't just be a believer, be a follower. Shane doesn't tell people to believe, he tells people to become 'followers of Christ', it's the following as much as believing that changes us. Love God, love others. Turn the other cheek, don't demand your rights. Help those in need whom you come across and share practical help when you can and the great message of Christ. Lastly find an alive church and throw yourself into that community of believers.

Following means a journey, and all journeys start with a first step, one foot moves forward, and that's it. Pray.

ABOUT THE AUTHOR

DAVID TAYLOR

David is a writer, television producer and director. He has also lectured in Journalism, Film, and Media at northern universities and colleges in the UK. After a rather misspent youth he settled down to a job in the Civil Service and then later started up in business. He was heavily involved in local politics during the 1980s before deciding to pursue the university education he missed when younger. After his graduation he stayed on to finish an MA in Cultural and Textual Studies and then started lecturing while working for a Phd. He started work in broadcast television as an independent producer with ITV in 1995. He wrote and produced a series of documentaries, 'Running Stories', inset within a magazine show for Tyne Tees Television, two of which helped the programme win 'Best Regional News Programme' in the 1996 Royal Television Awards, and a world medal in New York for 'Best News Magazine Programme'.

He says.

'For the record, although Shane and I share the same surname we are not related and didn't meet 'til three years ago. It's a real surprise that we hadn't met before as we both lived in Peterlee in the North-East of England. It isn't large – it was just around 8,000 strong when in 1963 I first came to a school in Peterlee from a pit village about six miles away. The town centre then was a single road, the cluttered sprawl of shops were all still to come, as were most of the housing estates. During my time there I had been a minister of a church, a district and town councillor, a failed businessman, and a late graduate to university.

'I say this because I know the town and have seen it grow, I ministered in a church three streets from where Shane lived at the time and know the community well. It has been a privilege to get to know him and I am continually impressed by his commitment to make a difference. I am honoured to write his story. It is an account that gives rise to so many questions, important questions about poverty, crime and the cycle of violence. It also gives important answers to those questions. It is also a story of redemption and leaves us knowing that if change can come to the life of Shane Taylor, change can come to anyone.'